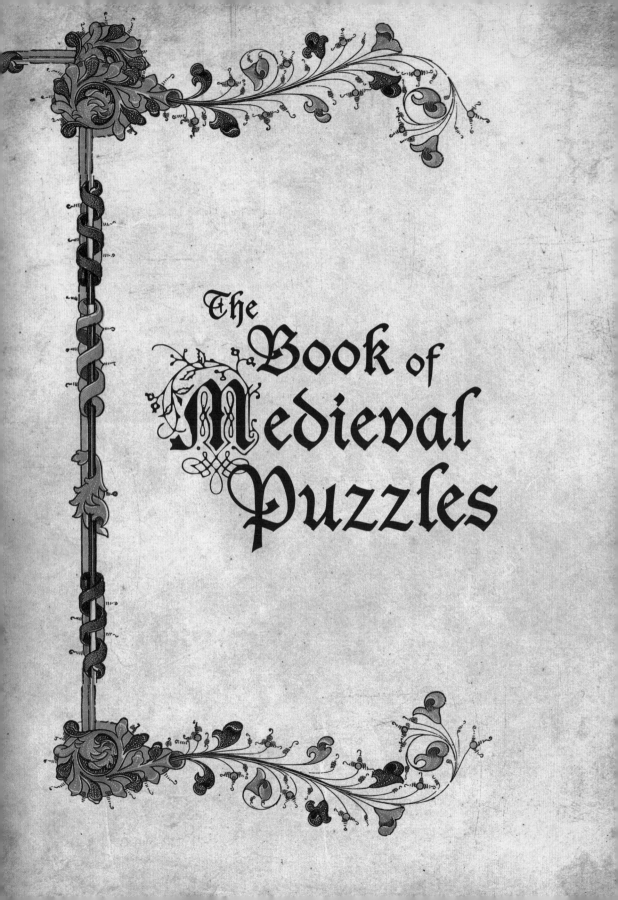

The Book of Medieval Puzzles

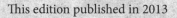

This edition published in 2013

by SevenOaks

20 Mortimer Street

London W1T 3JW

ISBN 978-1-78177-040-5

10 9 8 7 6 5 4 3 2 1

Printed in China

The Book of Medieval Puzzles

Being a fine and perplexing collection of conundrums, riddles and enigmas

By Tim Dedopulos

SEVENOAKS

Contents

Introduction   *8*

SIMPLE PUZZLES

MODERATE PUZZLES

TRICKY PUZZLES

HARD PUZZLES

Introduction

THE world changes, time upon time. The Florentine way spreads amongst us all, bringing mighty upheavals, and everything that I have known seems certain to be shaken to the very core. Perhaps this is natural, and Man ever looks behind with longing and forward with dread. If that is so, then I am no different. The tides of fate are sweeping in, crushing everything, and when they recede again, I cannot say what they will leave behind. I suspect, however, that kittens will be involved.

So, it falls to me, in this time and place, to make a record of that which is vanishing. It is a gargantuan undertaking, and it would be hubris itself to attempt to chronicle everything that there is. My particular love is for games of the mind, for trials of wit and wisdom and insight, for stern tests of mathematical reasoning and the Aristotelian logic of the Organon. Thus I have restricted my efforts to this field.

In this tome, I have endeavoured to collect a broad range of interesting puzzles and other problems. Civilisation spreads far and wide in these times, yet only a fool would discount the clever nature of the seemingly barbarous peoples – strange to our eyes, alas – that cluster outside its wings. You never know where an intriguing puzzle may be found. In exploring all possibilities, I feel that I have managed to assemble a pleasingly diverse selection of mental amusements. Some are arithmetical or geometrical, others matters of logic or insight. A few, indeed, are eminently practical. All of them have something to offer, I hope.

While on the topic of fondly optimistic anticipation, I feel I ought to at least acknowledge the possibility of this work surviving into posterity. Time is a ravening maw, in whose jaws we all are riven, mutilated and, inevitably, consumed. Its whimsies are utterly unfathomable. So, gentle reader, I cannot claim to know anything about you. Perhaps you are dear to me; or perhaps aeons have passed, and you have no form that I would even recognise as possessing awareness. The former seems far more likely. But, in case you are not able to ask me directly for elucidation,

I have attempted to make each problem in this volume is clear as my poor, feeble mind allows. Likewise, the solutions to each problem are as detailed and penetrable as it is in me to permit. If there is doubt or error, then it originates with my own clumsiness, and I beg forgiveness.

There are many ways to catalogue a selection of things, as every collector and librarian knows only too well. For this volume, I have attempted to group problems by the approximate level of challenge that they offer – to my mind, at least. No two brains are the same, and that which one person finds blindingly obvious, another of equal mental capacity may find utterly obtuse. But I have only my own mind to go on, and arranging in this manner – rather than by location, say, or alphabetic order – allows for a juxtaposition of theme and challenge which I myself find pleasing. I hope it likewise offers you some pleasure.

As the world totters on the brink of irrevocable and utter change, I say this to you, my familiar stranger: take heart in the human spirit. Time is pressing, true – but never so short that a moment of pleasure is a waste. We have made it this far. We will endure, and the future... the future will be wondrous.

AUTHOR'S NOTE

In compiling this book, I have treated history in the same way that a magpie treats a jewellery box – I've grabbed names, places, and other shiny nuggets of random fact, and woven them into the nest of my puzzles. In other words, it's safest to assume that I'm taking horrible liberties with anything that looks like it might be real information. I'm sorry about that. However, I hope you enjoy the puzzles.

- Tim Dedopulos, October 2012.

Simple puzzles

Barcelona

"OH, this won't do! This won't do at all!" The Seneschal to the Count of Barcelona was a small, nervous man, and he was clearly flustered.

"What is the matter?" The Seneschal's assistant, well used to his master's moods, managed to keep his voice patient, but he could not inject any concern.

"The Count is having a small, personal dinner engagement tonight. Everything must be perfect, and protocol is so variable!"

"Well, who is attending?" asked the assistant. "It cannot be that troublesome."

"Oh my! The Count is expecting his father's brother-in-law, his brother's father-in-law, his father-in-law's brother, and his brother-in-law's father."

"So there will be five," said the assistant. "Even allowing for niceties of status, that doesn't seem so stern."

"Oh, no, that is not at all correct," said the Seneschal, fanning himself. "That would be fine! But that is the very most people that it could be. The Count is expecting the very least!"

 The assistant peered at him suspiciously. "How many is that?"

Solution on page 179

Wise Man's Bluff

NCIENT legend dictated that unless the lord retained a certain number as advisers, the town would suffer disaster. Unfortunately, that number was clouded in vague language, and the Wise Men invariably disagreed with one another on every single topic under the sun. Simply greeting them with "Good morning" would lead to hours of impassioned argument. Asking them to agree on how many of their own number could be safely retired was utterly absurd.

The legend insisted that "The wise you must keep around you at all times. Without them, famine and pestilence will descend. They shall guard you by seeing all eventualities, in all manners of observation. Thus let there always be seven blind of both eyes, to see where sight cannot; two blind of one eye, to see in light and shadow; four with sight in both eyes, to clearly perceive danger; and nine that see with one eye, for the sake of clarity."

What is the smallest number of Wise Men that will fulfil the requirements?

Solution on page 179

Alcuin

ALCUIN, the Abbot of Marmoutier Abbey, was greatly fond of intellectual challenges, and had become known far and wide as a fierce scholar and teacher. One afternoon, he called his students into his office, and indicated to them five numbered sacks, which, he informed them, held grain.

"Pay attention," he said. "Each of these sacks contains a different amount of grain. Taken together, 1 and 2 weigh 12lbs. Similarly, 2 and 3 together weigh 13.5lbs. Numbers 3 and 4 weigh 11.5lbs. The last two sacks, 4 and 5, collectively weigh just 8lbs. Finally; it will be useful to know that sacks 1, 3 and 5 together weigh 16lbs.

What is the weight of each sack?"

Solution on page 179

13

Three Boatmen

HE master of a small marina on Saint Mark's Basin in Venice found himself faced with a particularly trying problem. Some equipment had been stolen, and the witnesses all disagreed vehemently with each other. One of the men was telling the truth, but the boat master could not tell which one it was.

Stripped of all the hand-waving and flowery insults, the three boatmen's claims could be summarised as follows:

Arrigo: "Benci is lying."

Benci: "Cipolla is lying."

Cipolla: "The other two men are both lying."

 Which one should the boat master trust?

Solution on page 180

Beam

AN architect, busily attempting to build a chapel, found that he needed to ensure that a beam was carefully balanced. If the alignment was off, the weight of the ceiling and arches would be improperly distributed, and disaster would undoubtedly ensue at some unfortunate point in the future.

This diagram summarises his problem – a beam of wood that has to bear two loads distributed unevenly from the point of balance. In this crude representation below, the marked divisions are all the same length. You can assume that the beam, rods and pivot point are rigid, and of negligible weight compared to the loads.

 If the left-hand load is fourteen hundredweight, what is the required right-hand load to keep the beam balanced?

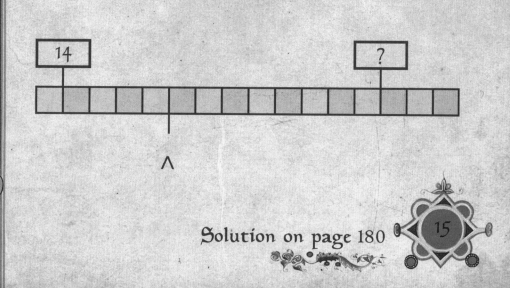

Solution on page 180

Equity

THE number 4 has fascinated theologians for centuries. Several Asian cultures consider the number 4 to be extremely unlucky, because their name for the number is very similar to their word for death.

It is a curious mathematical oddity that $2 + 2 = 2 \times 2 = 4$. Four is the only number that can be obtained by adding a number to itself and also by multiplying the same number by itself. However, there are many pairs of different numbers that can be both added and multiplied together to give the same answer.

Can you find the pair that total 4.5?

Solution on page 180

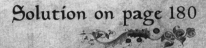

Roll Out

"ONE of the most important tasks I'll have for you," the innkeeper told his new cellar-boy, "is keeping track of how much ale and wine we have." He waved at the row of tall oak barrels along the cellar wall. "You need to be able to tell me when I get to half-way down a barrel, so I can start preparing its replacement. I don't want you using any filthy sticks in my beer, mind! You can take the lid off and look, nothing more. Ah, don't look like that, lad. Telling half-way is easy."

 So with no measuring device available other than your eyes, and no indicators inside a barrel, how would you work out when the barrel is half-empty?

Solution on page 181

Idiot

THE village of Whitchurch was home to a particularly celebrated idiot. He was well known throughout the region for always having the wrong idea about money. You see, whenever he was offered his choice of two coins, he would inevitably take the lowest-value one, and then cavort off, utterly delighted with his erroneous choice.

One clergyman in particular had trouble understanding why the fool behaved the way he did. He tried an entire range of combinations on the man, testing coins of different sizes, ages and even shininess. Although the poor wretch seemed to have no idea of the meaning of value, he still somehow managed to always take the option that would leave him worse off. In the end, the clergyman was able to rule out the coins' weight, thickness, diameter, colour, lustre, and even age as the factor that made the idiot invariably descend on the offering of lesser value. It certainly wasn't just abysmally bad luck.

 So how come the fool always took the less valuable coin?

Solution on page 181

18

Riddle-Me-Ree

N EVER speaking, still awake,
Pleasing most when most I speak,
The Delight of old and young,
Tho' I speak without a Tongue.
Nought but one Thing can confound me,
Many Voices joining round me;
Then I fret, and rave and gabble,
Like the Labourers of Babel.
I can bleat, or I can sing
Like the Warblers of the Spring.
Let the Love-sick Bard complain,
And I mourn the cruel Pain;
Let the happy Swain rejoice,
And I join my helping Voice.
Tho' a Lady, I am stout,
Drums and Trumpets bring me out;
Then I clash and roar, and rattle,
Join in all the Din of Battle.
Much I dread the Courtier's Fate,
When his Merit's out of Date,
For I hate a silent Breath,
And a Whisper is my Death.

Solution on page 181

19

Spot the Difference

HERE are ten differences between these two pictures.
Can you find them all?

Solution on page 182

A Serious Meal

ABBOT Alcuin was a very fair-minded and mathematically careful man. When the time came to provide a meal to five labourers that he had engaged to build a wall, he was rigorous about ensuring that each man received exactly the same.

This was simple enough with most of the food, but the bread was something more of a trial. Three round loaves had to be divided between the five men. To keep everything equal, each one must receive identical pieces to the others. To help avoid boring the men, they were not to receive more than one piece of any given size.

Meeting these terms as simply as possible, what pieces of bread did the men receive?

Solution on page 183

The Mason of Madrid

N enterprising Spanish mason with an eye for the mathematical had a curious design carved into the capstone of a well.

When asked about it, he would say only that it followed a certain undeniable logic, and that he had left it incomplete by way of a challenge.

What is the missing glyph?

Solution on page 183

Smelly Water

A TANNER of Girona was considering a range of methods for reducing the amount of 'dung water' he needed to soak the skins. It occurred to him that he could use less if he wrapped his skins around a wide rod before dunking them into the rancid bath.

"So," he said to himself, "let us start with a cylinder to hold the fluid, where every foot of depth holds a gallon of fluid. Then there needs to be a rod, so assume that that every foot of that is equal in bulk to half a gallon of liquid. It will need to be light. Then, wrapped in furs up to the four-foot mark, it is lowered into the dung water. Hmm. Four feet of rod would displace two gallons of water, so the cylinder will need to be two feet higher. But wait, the rod will be taking up space there as well. So the rod will then displace another gallon of dung water. This will again rise higher, and then the rod will displace it again, and then... Merciful God! It will never end, and I will be drowned in the foul stuff!"

Was he right to be worried?

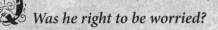

Solution on page 184

Birthday Boy

 MERCHANT was passing through the village of Wedendorf on his way to Wismar, and decided to spend the night at the inn. He had been relaxing by the fire for a while when one of the locals came over to him.

"You look like a clever fellow," said the local. "Explain the matter of my friend Kurt's age – he's over there – and we'll each buy you an ale. Fail, and you buy us one. Do we have a deal?"

Amused, the merchant agreed.

"It's like this," the local said. "Two days ago, Kurt was 34. Next year, he'll be 37, and that is the Lord's own truth. How can that be?"

What is the answer?

Solution on page 184

25

A Bed of Roses

 GARDENER bought nine roses to commemorate the nine years he had been married to his wife. He also wanted to celebrate the eight children they had together, so he came up with a clever idea.

 How would you plant them so as to end up with eight rows of roses, each row having exactly three flowers in it?

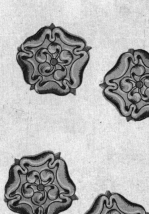

Solution on page 185

Looking Ahead

HREE men were sitting on separate tables in a market-side shisha house in Damascus.

They were the only patrons, for the working day was still on-going. Ibrahim was looking at Ahmed. Ahmed was looking at Sayeed. Sayeed, in his own turn, was carefully reading a bill of sale.

Now, Sayeed had hair of respectable length, carefully oiled and coiffured.

 If I reveal to you that it was Ibrahim's proud habit to honestly describe himself as being as bald as an egg, is it possible for you to tell me whether, amongst the patrons of the shisha house, a bald man is looking at a non-bald man?

Solution on page 185

The Ox

LI KAO sets off when the dawn rises to drive his number ten ox to the local market. The poor beast is laden with many catties of rice, and it is not, by temperament, inclined to any great exertion even under the best of circumstances. Li Kao manages to goad the animal to an average speed of 900 bu per kè. His efforts pay off, as he manages to sell all of his rice in a timely manner.

On the return journey, with all burdens relieved, there is a pleasant breeze at their backs. The prospect of some well-earned food and rest enlivens both man and ox. Consequently, Li Kao persuades his ox to achieve the dizzying average speed of 1500bu per kè.

In bu per kè, of course, what is the average speed for their journey?

Solution on page 186

Illumination

A MANUSCRIPT in the possession of a particular Abbot deviated from the typical fare by delving into tutelary matters. It included the following curious diagram:

$$\odot - \mathfrak{D} + \mathfrak{Y} = 7$$

$$\mathfrak{D} + \mathfrak{Y} \times \odot = 50$$

$$\mathfrak{Y} - \odot + \mathfrak{D} = 5$$

$$\mathfrak{D} \times \mathfrak{Y} + \odot = 29$$

 Assuming that calculations are performed in the order that they appear, what are the glyphs worth?

Solution on page 186

The Bag

A JEWELLER and a merchant were discussing the nature of blind chance. They had some fundamental differences in their opinions, and the jeweller found himself getting increasingly impatient. Finally, he proposed a trial.

"I have two small silk bags. Into the first, I have put a round stone. I will tell you now that it is either a pearl or a cheap bead, one as likely as the other. I have also done the same with the second bag. The bags may both hold pearls, or both hold beads, or one of each. Now, I am going to put what is definitely a pearl – here, you see? – into the second bag, shake it, and then pull out... Ah, a pearl. So the second bag is back down to one stone.

Now, my friend, without looking into either bag, is it possible to say which is more likely to contain a pearl?"

Solution on page 187

In the Village

OB and Bob were standing by the well, waiting to get some water, when Bob spotted a tall fellow he didn't recognise.

Bob squinted at the man, trying to place him. "Here, Hob, who's the stranger over there? The bloke with the ratty beard. He looks a bit familiar."

Hob snorted. "He's not a stranger. His mother is my mother's mother-in-law."

Bob looked at Hob suspiciously. "Eh?"

 Who is the man?

Solution on page 187

Magic Square

GERMAN philosopher Heinrich Cornelius Agrippa was one of the leading European mystics of the 16th century. In 1531, he expanded one of his previously published works to include the idea that various magic squares could be associated with heavenly bodies. The idea proved popular, and his squares, known as 'Kameas', are still a matter for discussion in modern times. In the square shown part completed below, every row, column and diagonal adds up to 65, and the numbers 1-25 appear once each. It is the square that Agrippa associated with the planet Mars.

 From the section provided, can you complete the square?

		7		
		25		
17	5	13	21	9
		1		
		19		

Solution on page 188

Matching Pairs

NLY one of the smaller designs matches the larger one in the centre. But which one?

A

C

B

D

Solution on page 188

33

The Blacksmith

OSÉ awoke one night to the unmistakeable noise of someone fumbling around in his smithy. He was a big man, the tallest and strongest in Pedraza. People who didn't know better thought him slow, but the truth was that he was cautious with his movements, to avoid causing harm. Sometimes, his image emboldened thieves, who might have been wiser hunting elsewhere.

Leaping out of bed with a furious bellow, José charged towards his front door. When he got outside, he could see the intruder fleeing up the street. José set off after him. The thief was quick, taking nine steps for each five strides that José managed, and he had a dozen steps by way of a head start. But thanks to his size, three of José's strides were worth five and a half of the thief's steps.

How far did José have to run to catch the thief?

Solution on page 190

May and June

AY lived in the town of Derby, with her sister June, and their mother. The sisters sold apples, and other fruits that became available from time to time. The pair was as identical as they were inseparable, which lent them certain fame around the town, and indeed they shared not only parents, but also the very hour of their birth. They dressed to increase the impact of their sameness, save that May always wore a red ribbon, and June a blue one – or at least, that was their claim, for there are times when an identical sister can be quite an advantage.

At least twice a day, some visitor to the town would see them and exclaim, as if it were a unique observation, "You must be twins!"

Their well-practised response was pitch-perfect, and utterly true. The two would look at the visitor, and in perfect synchrony arch an eyebrow and say, flatly, "We are most definitely not twins."

 Can you explain?

Solution on page 191

Firenze

HERE is a tree that sits at the centre of a very particular courtyard. Next to it is a statue, seven feet tall including the pedestal, which commemorates a very particular person. At a specific time on a specific day of the year, the shadows of the tree and the statue touch very particular points on a very specific design carved into the flagstones of the courtyard.

 At that moment... Hmm, perhaps I won't tell you what happens yet. Instead, I will tell you that the statue's shadow measures four feet in length, and the tree's shadow measures seven and a half feet, and maybe you will tell me the height of the tree?

Solution on page 192

The Templar Code

 FRENCH official apprehended a suspected Templar sympathiser shortly after the Order's dissolution. He had a number of documents on his person, several relating to the chartering of cargo boats to transport unnamed items to Scotland. All of the important details were encoded. However, one particular pair of sums caused the official great consternation. They involved the consistent substitution of certain numbers with encrypted designs.

One number was missing entirely. What was it?

```
              ♀    ♃    ☉    ×
                   ☉    ♃
        - - - - - - - - - - - - - -
   =    ♀    ♂    ☉    ♅    ♃    +
        ♀    ♂    ♄    ♅    ♃
        - - - - - - - - - - - - - -
   =    2    4    6    9    6


              ♂    ☽    ♃    ×
                   ?    ?
        - - - - - - - - - - - - - -
   =    ♀    ♆    ♀    ☽    ♄    +
        ♀    ♅    ♃    ♃    ☉
        - - - - - - - - - - - - - -
   =    3    4    2    3    6
```

Solution on page 192

One hump

A PAIR of camel traders were swapping shrewd observations on their relative ages during a quiet moment. "Mohammed," said the first, "you must surely realise that the numbers that make up your age are the same as those that make up mine, merely reversed." "Of course," said his companion. "Furthermore, the difference between our ages is precisely one eleventh of their sum."

 How old were the men?

Solution on page 193

Planking

ICHARD was watching his gaffer, Samuel, divide a plank into segments. Samuel sawed the plank exactly in half, clamped the two pieces together and sawed them both in half again, and then finally put all four bits in a pile and sawed them into eighths. Once he had dusted himself off, Samuel picked up one of the chunks and threw it to Richard.

"That was an 8-pound plank of oak, my lad," Samuel said.

Richard nodded. "Yep."

"So how much does that chunk weigh?"

"A pound," Richard said promptly.

Samuel snickered.

Why was Richard wrong?

Solution on page 194

Mine

HERE is something precious that you own.

You take it everywhere.

It weighs nothing but can carry weight.

You can share it with someone you haven't met.

Or even give it to someone you dislike.

Others may make more use of it than you do.

 What is it?

Solution on page 195

Good Morning

ONE of the smaller colleges of Bologna's famous university had a curious tradition. Every morning, after prayers, each student was required to bow to the headmaster, the tutors and every other student. Similarly, the tutors were required to bow to the headmaster, each other, and then the students in turn. The headmaster, naturally enough, bowed to no one.

Over the course of the morning greetings, 1296 bows were performed. Students outnumbered tutors eight to one.

How many tutors were there?

Solution on page 196

Sour Milk

"Lena!"

"Oh. Sofie."

"You're not still cross about that milk, are you? You shouldn't have left it there. Look, are you going to the Rathaus this afternoon? I think the Bürgermeister is going to make an announcement about the taxes."

"I am going."

"When is it happening?"

"Hmm. Four hours before the meeting is as far past four in the morning as it is before four in the afternoon."

"... Ah."

 When is the meeting?

Solution on page 196

Matching Pairs

 NLY one of the smaller designs matches the large one. Which one?

A

C

B

D

Solution on page 197

A Curious Design

 HIS glyph was found on a long-forgotten stone in the centre of a dark forest. The numbers surrounding it seem to suggest another.

 What number should be in the centre?

16

24   20

?

12   8

16

Solution on page 198

Marek

AREK had to travel to Knieja, a trip of several hours. Because he was low on funds, the coachman agreed to allow him a reduced fare, the condition being that if his place in the carriage was needed, he would have to sit up on the running bench with the coachman, out in the cold, rainy weather.

At first, all seemed well, as there was just one other man travelling. But half way through their journey, they picked up several more passengers and Marek had to join the coachman. He stayed up there, shivering, until he had only half as far to go again to Knieja as the distance for which he had been out in the cold. At that point, a passenger disembarked, allowing Marek back into shelter.

What proportion of the journey was Marek on the running bench for?

Solution on page 198

Needle's Eye

A MONK was in the town of Zaragoza, collecting charitable alms to help pay for the orphanage that his abbey provided. Having enjoyed some modest success, he came to the home of a minor member of the nobility, and despite some misgivings, decided to ask for a donation. The monk pled his case, and after some time, the lord's servant returned with a tattered scrap of filthy cloth, which he vehemently insisted the monk should take. He did so, and departed swiftly.

The following day, the Abbot sent a messenger back to the nobleman's house with sincere, enthusiastic declarations of his gratitude and appreciation.

 But why?

Solution on page 199

Premium Brandy

HE landlord of the Green Witch Inn in Trewissick, Bill Hoover, purchased most of his spirits from free traders – smugglers, to you and me. Supply of brandy was always erratic, so he was in the habit of preparing a blend he sold to his customers as 'premium'. Making the blend was fairly straightforward.

First of all, Bill got two casks. He emptied a standard keg of brandy into the smaller cask, and fresh water into the larger. Then he tipped water into the smaller cask until he had doubled its contents. The next step was to pour the mix back into the larger cask until he had doubled that one's contents. Finally, he used the liquid in the larger cask to refill his original keg. You'd never have found such shoddy treatment at Mevagissey House, that's for sure.

 How much brandy is in the old rogue's premium blend?

Solution on page 199

The Count

AMORAVIAN Count was widely known to be in ill health, having had a weak constitution since his childhood. Eventually he ordered the construction of a resting room, where he might enjoy conditions as tolerable as possible. It was to be thickly carpeted, warmed by generous fireplaces on the other side of its internal walls, and well-lined with bookcases and paintings. So that the Count would have a view, he insisted that a square window be put in, five feet high.

Once the room was completed, all was to the Count's satisfaction – apart from the window. It let in too much light. The Count called the builder back, and demanded that the man alter the window to let in half as much light. However, he refused to allow the poor builder to change the type of glass, or add a curtain, or a shade, or shutters, or otherwise do anything to impact the quality of the viewing. In fact, he insisted that the window had to stay five feet high, five feet wide, and square.

 Eventually, the builder came up with a method. What was it?

Solution on page 200

48

hundred Years

 MANY curious designs are to be found in the caves of the Dordogne. Some of these stem from the times when the region was home to the long, painful struggle between the English and the French. There were moments when it was important to ensure that information remained obscure.

What letters are missing from the third of these tablets?

3	8	5	2			
6	4	4	7	A	G	C
8	8	7	4			

5	9	0	1			
7	7	5	9	I	I	G
3	3	3	7			

7	3	9	6			
4	7	4	1	?	?	?
7	0	9	2			

Solution on page 200

 49

Cacciatore

A HUNTER was setting a snare in the woods when he spotted a large hare across a clearing. He whistled sharply to his dog, and pointed to it. The hare took off, with the dog in immediate pursuit. The dog was faster, and immediately started closing the distance.

The hare was 50 feet away when the chase started. If it took the dog 125 feet to catch the hare, how much further did the dog still have to run when there was just 30 feet between the two?

Solution on page 201

Infamy, Infamy

THE village elders gathered in the market square one evening to debate a knotty problem involving the behaviour of a young couple. One faction of the elders was scandalised, and felt that censure was the only option. The other faction was far less concerned, and wanted to leave the pair alone. Eventually, the unconcerned faction grew tired of the fuss, and wandered off.

It was noted in the alehouse across the way that if the woman who had called the meeting had decided to throw in with the unconcerned faction, then a full two thirds of the elders would have left. Alternatively, if she had been able to talk two of her regular cronies into staying with her, half of the meeting group would have still been there. As it was, neither of those things came to pass.

 How many people attended the meeting?

Solution on page 201

51

Moderate Puzzles

Three Jailers

THE Marienburg dungeons were rightly feared. Enemies of the Teutonic Order found little comfort there, and the chances of escape were minimal. Part of the forbidding reputation came from the constant vigilance of the jailers, of course.

The task of watching one of the corridors was shared by three low-ranking guards: Matthias, Bernt and Konrad. At least one of the men was to be attentively on duty at all times, on pain of the most horrible punishments. But there were other restrictions to be obeyed. If Matthias was off duty, and Bernt was off duty, Konrad would be on duty. However, any time that Bernt was off duty, Konrad would also be off duty.

 Could Matthias ever go off duty?

Solution on page 203

Rose Lines

 EN roses are arranged in two neat rows of five flowers each like so:

 By moving just four of the roses, can you arrange them into five rows of four flowers each?

Solution on page 203

The Calipha's Garden

 O Show his love for his wife, the Caliph of Baghdad decreed that a fabulous winding garden be constructed. It was almost square, just half a yard longer than it was wide, and divided entirely into the lanes of a single spiralling path. This mighty path, a yard wide throughout, was inlaid with semi-precious gems, and its edges were indicated with slender rods of copper. A great canopy of vines towered over everything, to provide shade. The path ended at the very heart of the garden, where a delicate fountain could be found.

Including the space taken up by the fountain, the path was a majestic 7788 yards in length. What were the dimensions of the garden?

Solution on page 204

55

The Pigs

I T was time for the Long Compton Pig Fair. Farmers far and wide drove their prize pigs to gather around the King's Stone overlooking the village, so that the judges could evaluate their swine.

Old Hob had been judging the fair for years, and was thoroughly bored of pigs, so he decided to speed it up a little this year.

Pigs were graded on appearance, weight and height, and he had a number of performance tokens that he could hand out among the animals he picked as finalists for detailed grading. These tokens were classed either 'bad' or 'good'. The same tokens were used for each of the three things a pig could be graded on Hob decided to hand out 'bad' in at least one category to either 9 or 10 pigs, 'bad' in at least two categories to 4 or 5 pigs, and the wooden spoon of the finalists, three 'bad' tokens, to 2 or 3 pigs. Similarly, 8 or 9 pigs would get at least one 'good' token, 3 or 4 would get two 'good' tokens, and just one pig would be crowned the winner with three 'good' tokens.

Assuming that each finalist has to get at least one token, what's the least number of pigs that Hob can get away with giving tokens to, and what is the greatest number of tokens he can distribute among them?

56

Solution on page 205

Three Squares

 N old monastery on the foothills of the Hua Shan was reputed to be as ancient as time itself. One of its most remarkable features was an odd design, carved deep into the stone floor of a small chamber, and set deep in the rock below the rest of the monastery. It was said that to walk the design in one continuous path, without ever treading the same line twice, was to open oneself to enlightenment. Of course, no one ever claimed that attaining enlightenment was easy.

Can you see a way?

The Top of the hill

THE Grand Old Duke of York was said to have ten thousand men. That is a respectable army, no doubt, but there have been many that have been considerably larger, both before and after. In France, a prince raised an army that consisted of 187 squadrons of cavalry and 207 battalions of infantry. Each squadron held four companies of 39 riders, and was commanded by a lieutenant colonel. Each battalion extended to three companies of 186 men, and was led by a colonel, assisted in turn by a lieutenant colonel.

Assuming that officers above the rank of colonel would rather not get their hands dirty, and that some 473 soldiers are presently incapacitated through illness, how many men can the prince send into battle?

Solution on page 207

Quite Contrary

ALKING into a flower garden, Lorenzo spotted a group of lovely young women taking their morning ease. Wishing to make an extravagant impression, he declared, "Upon my life! Ten pretty maids, all in a row. Such beauty I did never hope to spy."

The young women shared a glance. "Sir," said one of them, "your eyes deceive. We are not actually in a row, and furthermore there are not ten of us. However, if we were twice as many again as we are, we should be as many above ten as we are presently under that number."

"I see," said Lorenzo, and somewhat abashed, he took his leave.

 How many ladies were there?

Solution on page 207

Reales

W HEN Ernesto married Maria, her dowry came in the form of her wedding gown. Her dress was strung with bandoliers of silver bells that tinkled beautifully as she walked.

There were four bandoliers in total, each one holding 27 bells. Although equally lovely, the bells were of differing sizes. Just less than a fifth were small, worth just 3 reales, and just under half that many were large, worth 8 reales. The remainder were of an in-between size, valued at 5 reales.

How much was Maria's dowry worth?

Solution on page 208

Potato Farming

ANS was helping his father, Kurt, plant potatoes. After a while, his father put the basket down and called Hans over.

"My son," Kurt said, "Tell me something. Imagine I were to ask you to bring a barrel of 100 potatoes to this spot. Then, I instruct you to take the potatoes out one at a time, and plant them a yard apart in a straight line, starting one yard from the barrel and leading away down the field. After each planting, you would come back to the barrel, and take another potato if one remained."

"My father," Hans said, "You can imagine I would tell you precisely what to do with your potatoes."

 Can you calculate how many yards Hans would have to walk to achieve such a thing?

Solution on page 209

Spot the Difference

HERE are ten differences between these two pictures, can you find them all?

Solution on page 210

Black or White

"ON the table before you, there is a bag."

"Yes, I see it."

"Four counters are inside it. Each of the four may be either black or white, but they are otherwise identical. Without looking draw out two of them."

"Very well. A moment... They are both white."

"Excellent. What do you think the chance of drawing a third white counter to be?"

"Well..."

"Hold a moment. I meant to tell you that there was at least one white counter in the bag to start with."

"Ah! That makes all the difference!"

Does it really?

Solution on page 211

The Mathematical Mason

CERTAIN Madrileño Mason discovered that an enigmatic well cover he had prepared had become the source of some speculation. Finding this fact to be rather amusing, he decided to do something similar with the lid of a large storage trough he was working on.

 Can you complete the pattern?

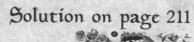

Balance

HE process of constructing a building is a delicate one. The proper balance of loads is vital. Without it, structures do not stay standing for very long.

In this crude representation below, a tricky issue of balance is reproduced as simply as possible. The marked divisions are all the same length. You can assume that the beam, rods and pivot point are rigid, and of negligible weight compared to the loads, which are given in hundredweight.

 What value is required to balance the beam?

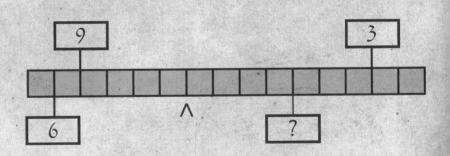

Solution on page 212

The Ale Yard

HE Green Witch Inn in Trewissick was known more for the cheap cost of its drinks than for their quality. They were certainly good value, which helped to offset the landlord's surly nature, and there was often less violence amongst the patrons than you might have found in other low-budget pubs.

The reason, of course, was that the landlord had a habit of watering down the ale. His standard practice was to fill a large jug from a ten-gallon keg, and fill the keg back up with water. Setting aside the pure ale for his own consumption, he would then fill the jug a second time with the weakened ale, which he sold at a slightly higher price, and again fill up the large keg with water. By the time he had done this, the mix in the keg was exactly 50% beer and 50% water.

 What size was the jug?

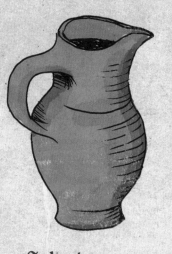

Solution on page 212

67

In Norfolk

WORD quickly spread round the port town of King's Lynn. It turned out that Tom Mears, who had recently died, had in fact been married to the sister of his own widow! Folk shook their heads, and wagged their fingers, but the truth of it was inescapable.

But how?

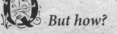

Solution on page 213

Bucket List

A CARTER'S apprentice, stricken with curiosity one lunchtime, had part-filled a large bucket with water, and then floated a smaller bucket inside the larger. The water level rose, leaving the smaller bucket partly submerged.

As he was peering at it, the carter came past, and paused for a moment. "Do you see, lad? The floating bucket pushes aside enough water to equal its bulk." He wandered off again.

The apprentice looked at the buckets doubtfully. "But it's full of air. How can that be true?"

Solution on page 213

69

The hunter's Spears

 TAKE a look at these columns of numbers. The left one adds to 19, and the right one adds to 20. It is possible, by moving one pair of numbers, to have both columns add to the same total.

 How is it done?

1	3
2	4
7	5
9	8

Solution on page 215

Ivan the Rather Unpleasant

VAN Dolovich fancied himself to be an important man. So what if the other merchants of Rovnoye did not agree? Having left a seemingly interminable meeting with some impertinent trappers, he found himself unsure of how much time had passed.

An uncouth fellow was passing, so Ivan Dolovich stepped into the man's path, and said, "I, Ivan Dolovich, need to be informed of the correct time."

The man, clearly not expecting such interaction, recoiled. Once he had regained his balance, he eyed Dolovich coolly. "I find your plight keenly distressing. Allow me to rectify such vicious injustice. Clearly, a masterful intellect such as yours will understand me precisely when I inform you that if you take a quarter of the current elapsed time since midday today, and a half of the time remaining between now and midday tomorrow, and add these two values together, you will have the correct time."

"Clearly," replied Dolovich weakly.

 What time is it?

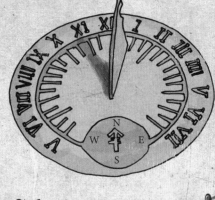

Solution on page 215

Spot the
Difference

HERE are ten differences between these two pictures. Can you find them all?

Solution on page 216

The Battle Of Grunwald

THE Battle of Grunwald went very badly for the Teutonic Knights. Poland and Lithuania combined forces to flatten them. Many men were lost that day, including the Grand Master himself, and although the Teutonic Knights survived as an order, their power never recovered.

Some time after the battle, when the Hospitaller of the Knights had divided the survivors into convenient groups, he sent his juniors to survey the injuries that the men had suffered. One of the reports was somewhat less thorough than he had hoped.

"Out of 100 men," said the lad, "64 have lost at least part of a limb, 62 are unable to grasp a weapon, 92 are unable to stand unaided, and 87 show signs of infection."

What is the minimum number of men unlucky enough to have all four problems?

Solution on page 217

Operators

BSERVE the following set of numbers:

$$1\ 2\ 3\ 4\ 5\ 6\ 7\ 8\ 9 = 100$$

This statement can be made mathematically accurate by placing just three simple numerical operators – that is, one or more of +, -, × and ÷. You cannot change the position of any of the digits, but you should treat any digits not separated by an operator as one number. In other words, 1+2 3 would be "1 + 23", while 1 2÷3 would be "12 ÷3."

 Can you solve the statement?

Solution on page 217

Cassie

CASSIE always wore practical shoes. They might not have been particularly lovely, but they were well-fitting and hard-wearing, and it would be fair to say that she hardly noticed them most of the time.

In fact, the truth is that she never took them off – not even to go to sleep at night – until she literally outgrew them. Even then, her next pair was always close to identical to the old ones. She truly wasn't obsessive about them, however.

Can you explain?

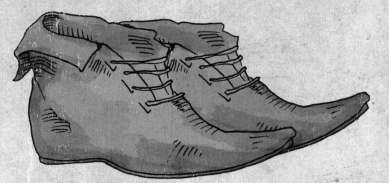

Solution on page 218

Monkey Puzzle

ATHER close, my friends, gather round! I have a true marvel for you here. Yes, that's right, come up nice and close. Manel, the lovely lady monkey patiently clinging to the rope, has come to us all the way from far Takrur, and she is my invaluable assistant. My other equally invaluable assistant, Karim, is sitting over there. Oh, don't look like that, Karim. He doesn't like being reminded that he's as important as a monkey, my friends, but truly I am no more important than either of them.

The rope, as you can see, passes over a wheel and back down to a lump of genuine star-metal. It fell from the heavens, and when evil is near, it has been known to let out a chilling whine. And it is silent now! No evil here. But more importantly, it is the exact same weight as my beloved Manel. What you cannot see is the amazing cleverness inside my wheel, the finest in all Marrakesh, which allows the rope to move completely freely.

When I give the signal, Manel will start to climb the rope.

Cheer poor, sad Karim up by allowing him the privilege of taking your bets, and feel free to help yourself to a juicy date at the same time.

Now, my friends, what will happen with the weight? Will Manel or the star-metal reach the top first?

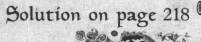

Solution on page 218

Always

T is a simple truth that, throughout all of history, some things stay the same. And so it is here.
    In this sum, the numbers from 0 to 9 have been replaced with letters, so that the same letter always represents the same number.

 If I tell you that none of the numbers shown begin with a zero (0), can you tell me the final total?

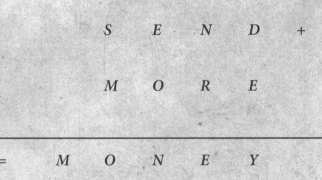

Solution on page 218

Alhambra

A MERCHANT in the Sierra Nevadas needed to make a delivery to the Alhambra. His route there took him along a flat road for a while, and then up a hill; his return journey took the same route. The actual delivery of his goods took just an instant.

On level ground, his pace was 4 miles per hour. Uphill, it dropped to 3 mph; downhill, it was 6 mph. He started his journey at 8am, and returned home at 2pm, before the worst of the day's heat.

To within 30 minutes, at what time did he drop off his delivery?

Solution on page 219

Meissen

THE Margrave of Meissen wanted his sons to gain some fluency in numbers, so he had created for them a magnificent set of illustrated plaques, one for each of the numbers from 1 to 9. These he presented with a stern admonishment to care, and a challenge. Using all nine of the plaques, and nothing else, the task was to assemble four separate square numbers.

 Could you do it?

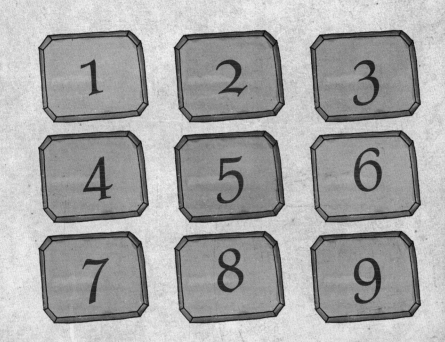

Solution on page 220

Old Tom

 OW old are you really, Old Tom?"
"That would be telling, my dear. But maybe you can figure it out for yourself. In six years' time, I'll be one and a quarter times as old as I was four years ago."

 How old is Old Tom?

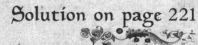

Solution on page 221

Scaling

VERY merchant understands the importance of being able to measure the weight of an object. Weighing scales have been at the heart of mercantile endeavour for almost as long as human civilisation. How else is fairness to be obtained, other than through balance?

The diagram below represents several sets of weighing scales. Each of the scales is properly balanced, so that the weight of one side is equal to the weight of the other.

Taking the smallest whole-unit values, what does each symbol weigh?

$$\odot \; \mathbb{D} \;\; = \;\; \yen$$

$$\mathbb{D} \; \mathbb{D} \; \odot \;\; = \;\; \varphi$$

$$\yen \; \yen \; \yen \;\; = \;\; \varphi \odot \mathbb{D} \odot$$

$$\yen \; \varphi \;\; = \;\; \mathbb{D} \odot \mathbb{D} \odot \mathbb{D}$$

Solution on page 221

The heist

A GROUP of rough-and-ready types spent several long days in the taverns of Southampton's dock district, making plans. This included long periods watching one particular warehouse, owned by a respected wine merchant. After all their plotting was complete, the men waited until the small hours of the morning, then broke into the warehouse, overpowered the guard, and absconded with several hundred casks of extremely expensive spirits.

The next morning however, the guard and the merchant were arrested, and the men were not. Why was that?

Solution on page 222

The Courier

HILE travelling the rural route from Briccolino to Cortanze, a young courier from Torino found himself with something of a problem. Not being familiar with the country, he relied upon the signposts along the way.

At one particularly complex five-way junction, he discovered that the signpost had fallen down, and he had no idea which road led onwards to Cortanze.

What should he do to help himself find his way?

Solution on page 222

Matching Pairs

NLY one of the smaller images matches the large one. Which one?

A

B

C

D

Solution on page 223

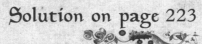

85

The Moneylender

A MONEYLENDER stood before the King, accused of being dishonest in his business transactions.

The King asked him:

"How much larger is four fourths than three fourths?"

"Why a fourth, your majesty." replied the moneylender.

A simple answer to a simple question. But the King banished the moneylender from his Kingdom.

 Why?

Solution on page 224

For the Cheese

OR the sake of argument, let us say that Schoonhoven, known for its beer, is directly south of the hamlet of Mijdrecht. Gouda, rightly celebrated because of its creamy cheese, is about twelve miles to the west of the north-south line between Schoonhoven and Mijdrecht, and closer to Schoonhoven than it is to Mijdrecht.

Travelling from the latter to the former, you find that your route takes you via Gouda. Calculating only straight-line distances, the journey via Gouda is 35 miles in length.

How far is it from Mijdrecht to Schoonhoven if you were to go directly?

Solution on page 225

The heralds

SIR Oswald rides out from York to Lincoln, his horse travelling at a consistant eight miles per hour. Sir Edmund sets out from Lincoln on the road to York at exactly the same time; his steed travels at nine miles per hour but must stop every two hours for a five minute rest.

When the two knights meet, who will be closest to Lincoln, Sir Oswald or Sir Edmund?

Solution on page 226

Witchcraft

HIS odd tablet was found in the home of a suspected witch in Seville. It breaks into four identically-shaped pieces, each containing precisely one of each of the six symbols.

 Can you see how?

♌		♏			♉
		♏			
	♋		♋		♌
	♊		♊		♈
♊		♋	♋	♈	♈
♊	♈	♉		♏	♏
				♌	♌
	♉	♉			

Solution on page 227

Saintly

A YOUNG lady of the town of Nyen on the river Neva was the object of much attention within the town. This was partly due to her father's status as an Överstelöjtnant of Nyenskans fortress, and partly due to her loveliness and keen mind.

With most of the town's eligible bachelors to choose from, she was given to offering tests to would-be suitors. One such test involved the age of her eldest brother. She had fourteen siblings, born eighteen months apart on average.

The eldest, her aforementioned brother, was eight times the age of the youngest. How old was he?

Solution on page 228

Diptych

A FLEMISH painter of some renown was in the habit of encoding mysterious glyphs and tables within his masterpieces. This particular curious arrangement appeared in one of them, painted so as to appear carved into the wall of a cave.

What value does each symbol have?

	27	26	28	25	
37	☉Ƴ	☽☉	ƳƳ	ƳƳ	37
38	ƳƳ	Ƴ☉	☽Ƴ	☉☉	38
31	☉☽	☽Ƴ	Ƴ☉	Ƴ☽	31
	27	26	28	25	

Solution on page 228

P It's a Trap

A PAIR of horse-pulled traps regularly travels both ways along a particularly scenic section of the bank of the Vltava river in Praha. The journey takes a quarter of an hour, so the traps simultaneously depart in each direction every fifteen minutes.

A man walking the same route starts off on foot at the same time as a trap does. Twelve and a half minutes later, he meets one coming the other way.

How much longer will it be before he is overtaken by that trap on its journey back out?

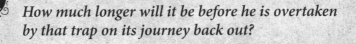

Solution on page 229

The Courtyards

A LARGE home in Toledo was built so as to consist of rooms around four courtyards, arranged as a square. Decorative gardens filled the space between. The buildings were constructed with an arrangement of numbers carved in place on the roofs, and inlaid into the statue at the heart of each courtyard.

 What is the number in the fourth courtyard?

3	4	3	9
8			12
7	6	5	5
7	2	8	1
7		?	
4	6	5	4

Solution on page 229

Tricky Puzzles

Shares

S a matter of educational discipline, Bishop Alcuin decided to put a group of ten novices to the test. He explained to them that their portions of dinner that evening would be combined into one, and then divided unequally. Specifically, he was going to rank the novices by the time they took to correctly complete a task. The person who came first would get the largest share and each following person's share would be ⅛ of a normal portion smaller than the one above it.

The task was to answer a question: what would be the size of the largest and smallest shares of dinner, measured in portions?

Solution on page 231

The Woodcutter's Sons

THE woodcutter's three sons were hearty young men, blessed with significant amounts of strength and generally pleasant temperaments. On the 21st birthday of one of the brothers, a visitor commented that the ages of two of the three added together was equal to double the third.

The woodcutter nodded, and then said that at one point, two of their ages added had been equal to the third. Not to be outdone, the son whose birthday it was pointed out that their total combined age, on that earlier occasion, was one and a half times greater than the number of years that had passed since then.

How old are the sons?

Solution on page 232

The Quad

HE residential student dormitories of one of the stranger colleges of a famous English university were built as large, square buildings with generous internal courtyards. Each set of rooms had a door onto the courtyard, which was otherwise inaccessible. There were eighty sets of rooms opening onto it in total, their doors evenly spaced to divide each wall of the courtyard into 21 identical sections. The sets of rooms were numbered from 1 at the top left, looking at the building on a standard map, and counted round clockwise back to number 80.

One evening, the students in numbers 9, 25, 52 and 73 engaged in a wager as to whose rooms were closest to the other three, where closest meant "the shortest sum of the three straight-line differences from doorway centre to doorway centre."

 Which students' rooms are closest to the others?

Solution on page 233

Digimancy

 UMBERS can be very magical things. Even the ancient druids understood the truth of this. There is a six-digit number that, when multiplied by 2, 3, 4, 5 or 6, remains made up of the same digits in the same order. All that changes is the place where the number starts.

Can you find out what it is?

Solution on page 234

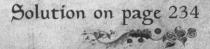

The Maze

TART at the centre. You are allowed to weave over or under other paths, but a single line cutting the path represents a dead end.

 Can you find a way to escape from this maze?

Solution on page 235

Nuremberg

HORTLY after the Peace of Nuremberg, a skilled artificer of metals was examining a clock. Coming to a realisation, he called his assistant over.

"Manfred, see here. The positions of the hands on this device are interlinked."

"Yes, Herr Müller?"

"There are some times of the day when the two hands might be interchanged and still be in correct positions for some other time, but usually that will not be the case. So, for instance, at 6 o'clock, you have the hands vertically aligned, but swapping them round, to indicate 12.30, would be incorrect, because at 12.30, the hour marker is not vertical, it is half-way between 12 and 1 on the dial."

"I see."

"I need you to calculate how many such pairs of positions there are on the clock face."

 Can you do it?

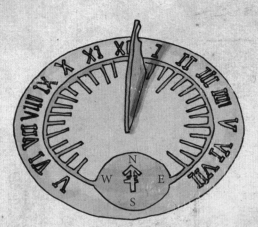

Solution on page 236

The Templar Treasure

WORD came down to the Knights Templar that Philip the Fair was about to have his tame Pope declare them heretics, in an attempt to seize their wealth. Their first priority was to ensure the survival of the order. Therefore, their holy relics and other valuables had to be moved out of his reach. Everything important was packed up tight to be shipped to the court of King James in Scotland, who was disinclined to listen to France or Rome.

The gold bullion they possessed had already been cast into slabs, 11" wide, 12.5" long, and 1" deep. These were packed into trunks 800 at a time, each trunk to be guarded by a squad of the fiercest knights that the order possessed. It is interesting to note that the trunks were square, and just high enough to hold the slabs with no wasted space left over. Less than a dozen slabs had to stand on edge, even. The trunks were so mighty that they were filled in place on specially reinforced carts that were hauled straight onto the waiting boats at Saint Malo, teams and all.

When Philip the Fair came calling, all he found were a few old men and the order's Grand Master, Jacques de Molay. The Templars, and their treasure, vanished into the shadows of history.

But what were the dimensions of the trunks, in inches?

Solution on page 237

The Keg

A CARTER, a hauler and a cooper had just finished a long and demanding job for a brewer, ensuring that the pubs of the local area all had plenty of his ale. Because the work had gone well, and swiftly, the brewer rewarded them with a six-quart keg of his finest to split between them. Unfortunately, when they sat down together to broach it, they realised that the only clean vessels they had available were a 5-pint bucket and a 3-pint stone jar.

How could they divide and consume their beer fairly?

Solution on page 238

The Prisoner

S has been mentioned before, the dungeons at Marienburg were a terrible place. The most horrible chambers were reserved for traitors. The oubliettes were cramped, filthy pits with a narrow opening at the top, the only source of light and air. If the fall into the oubliette didn't kill you, eventually the isolation would. Those who managed to avoid a broken limb tried to climb out, of course. The top was barred, but even so, they tried.

One particular prisoner tried to climb to the top every day. The walls were slightly sloped, but even so, the effort was very tiring. He had to stop and rest every five minutes, and invariably, during his rest, he would slip a yard down the wall. During his first burst of climbing, he would get two yards up, but each subsequent effort would get him only 90% as far as the time before.

Given that he needed to climb four and a half yards to get to the top, how many bursts of climbing did it take before he either hit the top or had reached his maximum height?

Solution on page 239

Trouble in France

DOCUMENTS seized from a Templar sympathiser after the Order's suppression contained a series of encoded mathematical operations. These caused particular consternation among Philip the Fair's agents, as they suspected that these had some bearing on the Order's fabulous wealth. The King was extremely angry that he had not managed to get his hands on it, and the agents were desperate to trace it.

Can you translate the coded numbers and find the missing one?

			⛢	♄	♀	×
			♀	♇		
			—	—	—	—
=	♂	♄	☽	♂	♃	+
	♂	⛢	♂	☉	♆	
	—	—	—	—	—	—
=	2	9	9	4	9	

			☽	♇	♀	×
			?	?		
			—	—	—	—
=	♆	♀	♂	♀		+
	♇	♀	♂	♀	☉	
	—	—	—	—	—	—
=	6	3	5	7	9	

Solution on page 239

104

Shadows

NLY one of the mirrored silhouettes matches the image on the left. Which one?

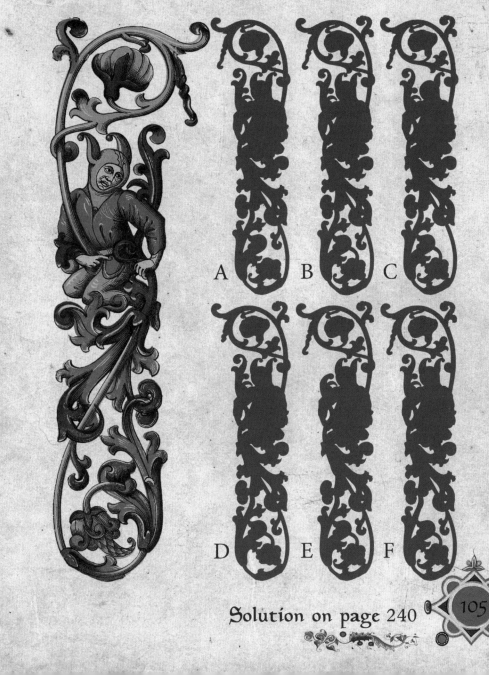

A   B   C

D   E   F

Solution on page 240

Dealing

DEALER of antiquities in Tyre was pleased and surprised to be able to sell a rather ugly statuette for the very generous price of ten Ashrafi darahim. In fact the purchaser, an older gentleman, barely haggled at all. Once the purchase had been completed, the delighted customer informed the dealer that the statuette was in fact one of an identical pair, together worth many times the amount he had paid. He informed the dealer that if he could find the other piece, he would cheerfully pay ten times as much for the second statue.

Later that day, the dealer started making some casual enquiries about the possibility of there being another statuette. Four days later, a man arrived at his shop with a statuette that was indeed identical to the first. He offered it to the dealer for thirty Ashrafi darahim.

Should the dealer buy the statuette?

Solution on page 241

Leonardo's Balls

DURING the Renaissance, Italy was a very exciting place to be. It was a time of artistic and scientific triumph, summed up by the life of perhaps the greatest genius that mankind has yet known – Leonardo da Vinci. Of course, not every discovery made during that time was earth-shatteringly significant.

Imagine that you have a very heavy ball, with a very light ball balanced precisely on top of it, both made of perfectly elastic materials. You drop the balls, from the height of 1 foot, onto a hard stone floor.

How high will the very light ball bounce?

Solution on page 242

Alice

"HAVE you seen Tom Worth's younger sister? Charming, she is."

"Alice. Yes. She's a bit on the clever side, you know. I asked her how old she was now. The answer fair took my breath away."

"Why?"

"Well, apparently Tom is twice as old as Alice was when Tom was half as old as Alice will be when she is three times as old as Tom was when he was three times as old as her. Oh, and together they come to 44 years."

"God's Teeth! What did you say to that?"

"I wished her a long life and bid her farewell."

 How old is Alice?

Solution on page 243

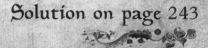

Rum Business

MANY a landlord, in times past, has resorted to watering the drinks they sold as a way of making the stock go further. But there have always been times when it was simply not safe to attempt such shenanigans. As Bill Hoover, landlord of the Green Witch Inn in Cornwall knew all too well, you didn't risk watering smugglers' rum. Violent men they were, and pitiless. No, you used cheap red wine instead.

So when he was preparing service for the fair traders, Bill would get a couple of large jugs, and put a quart of rum in one, and a quart of wine in the other. Then, making sure not to spill so much as a drop at any point, he would carefully perform the following routine: Transfer three ladles of rum into the wine. Stir thoroughly, and transfer two ladles from the wine jug back to the rum. Stir thoroughly again, and transfer a ladle from the rum jug to the wine jug. Finally, transfer a further two ladles from the wine jug to the rum jug, without stirring. Then he would sell the contents of the rum jug to the smugglers as 'real rum, lads, the proper stuff,' and the contents of the wine jug to everyone else as 'genuine rum.'

But was there more rum in the wine jug or more wine in the rum jug?

Solution on page 244

Grand Designs

 HIS glyph, like its cousin, was found etched into an ancient stone, half-buried in the mossy floor of a forest.

 What number should be in the middle?

14

38

9

?

3

11

13

Solution on page 244

Crossed Lines

 SMALL fort in the hills was known for having two flagpoles of quite radically different heights. One was just five ells tall, whilst the other stood an impressive 17 ells. In addition to the flags, wires were strung from the top of each pole to the foot of the other, and the spot where they crossed was bound round with wire, and used to hold a depiction of the captain's coat of arms.

How high were the wires when they crossed?

Solution on page 245

Embroidery

HONOR was practising embroidery with Elena, Georgina and Ana. She noted that Georgina was the same relation to Elena as she herself was to Ana. Furthermore, Honor herself held the same relationship to Elena as Georgina has to her.

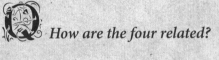 *How are the four related?*

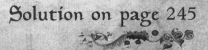

Solution on page 245

It's Time

 IFTY-FIVE minutes ago, it was three times as many minutes past 4.30pm as it now is before 7pm.

 What time is it?

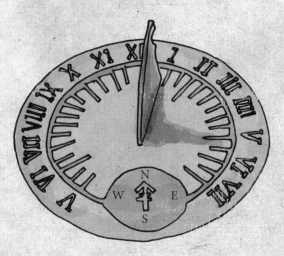

Solution on page 246

113

Century

GIVEN the long history of conflict that has afflicted the region, people in the Dordogne have often needed to make sure that they kept certain bits of information secret from enemy forces. The designs reproduced below, taken from tablets found in caves around the region, reflect that need for secrecy. In them, the letters are related mathematically to the numbers.

 What letters are missing from the third tablet?

9	1	6	1			
2	3	9	5	A	G	C
9	8	8	1			

7	5	7	8			
3	6	9	4	A	H	B
4	9	7	2			

4	2	6	1			
3	9	4	5	?	?	?
8	1	5	7			

Solution on page 246

Run, Rabbit

ROUGH-LOOKING fellow was being chased by a collection of furious, well-armed men. Having left them behind for a moment, he glanced around quickly, and then made a jump for the prison wall. He was more athletic than he looked, and within a few seconds he made it to the top. He leapt down to the other side, breathed a sigh of relief, and immediately went looking for a town guard.

Why would he do that,
having just successfully escaped?

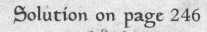

Solution on page 246

Rose Crux

OU find yourself in possession of a ring of nine roses.

Can you arrange them so as to form precisely nine lines of three roses each?

Solution on page 247

Shafir

MAR Shafir was a dealer in exotic perfumes and unguents. When he died, his three sons inherited 30 valuable ornamental jars, to be divided equally between them. Ten of the jars were full of precious incense, ten more were half-full, and the remaining ten were empty.

How are the jars to be distributed so that each son gets ten vessels, five full measures of incense, and at least one of each of the three types of jar?

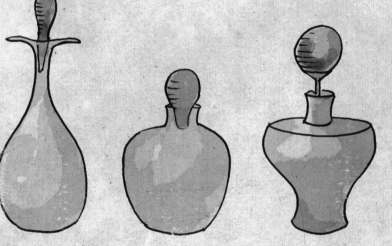

Solution on page 247

On The Road

COURIER was riding along a rural road in Provence when he spotted a farmer standing in a broad hole, and digging. The courier paused, curious. "You seem to be rather deep already, Sir. How far down are you planning to dig?"

The farmer looked up at him. "It's for the sheep," he said, and the courier thought he detected an ominous glint in the man's eye. "It's a third done, and when it's finished, my head's going to be twice as far below the ground as it is above it right now. And I'm five foot ten."

"Excellent work," said the courier nervously. He rode off, in case the man decided to tell him the pit's exact purpose.

How deep was the hole?

Solution on page 248

Scaled

BALANCE is a state to be admired. In it, one may find fairness, justice, even at times a hint of perfection. This is particularly true in trade, for an imbalance, left unchecked, will tip the scales so far that everything is lost. It's an important lesson to remember.

The scales below are all in perfect balance.

Taking the smallest whole-unit values, what does each symbol weigh?

$$\text{☿ ☽} \quad = \quad \text{☿ ☉ ☿ ☉}$$

$$\text{☽ ☽} \quad = \quad \text{☉ ☿ ☉ ☉ ☿ ☉}$$

$$\text{♀ ☿ ♀} \quad = \quad \text{☉ ☽ ☉ ☽ ☉}$$

Solution on page 248

The Marmo Set

T was a day of celebration in the Marmo household, as it was the 21st birthday of the eldest daughter, Luisa. When the various guests had arrived, the children were presented to them in order, from youngest to oldest. First, Norina was introduced, followed quickly by her brother Biagino. The children's aunt turned to her own daughter and said, quietly, "He's twice her age, you know." Then it was the turn of Erminia, the middle sister. "Ah! But she brings the girls' age combined to exactly twice Biagino's age now," said the aunt. Her daughter rolled her eyes.

When the older son, Salvatore, arrived, the aunt cheerfully declared that the boys' ages now doubled the girls again. Finally, Luisa was brought in, so the party could start. "The girls double the boys, at the end," said the aunt, but her daughter was already making a beeline for the pastries.

How old are the five Marmo children?

Solution on page 248

Alignment Issues

ERR Barras of Geneva was studying an impressive clock face. The machinery was inactive, with the hands pointing to precisely 8 o'clock. His friend, Herr Weber who was standing next to him, said, "Why are the two sticks not together?"

"Then it wouldn't be 8 o'clock," said Herr Barras.

"No, it would be 12 o'clock."

"Not necessarily." Herr Barras shrugged. "The hands come together several times."

Herr Weber frowned at him.

"So what's the next time after 8 o'clock that both sticks are exactly together?"

Solution on page 249

Calne

IN Calne, I came across a most peculiar sight. Evidence of a miracle, the fellow said. The work of the Saints, according to his claim. Well perhaps, but then again, perhaps not. The marvel in question was an egg, shell utterly unblemished, inside a bottle that was clearly too small to allow its egress.

How could such a thing be possible?

Solution on page 250

high Stakes

TWO rivals sat facing each other across a square table, two feet to each side. Each was armed with a very large number of identical wooden stakes, four inches long, flat at one end, and with a ¼-inch tip at the other, which tapered evenly to a point.

The honour and respect of the entire village was, well, at stake. The winner would be the last person to place a stake onto the table without disturbing any other stakes; the only other rule was a prohibition on interfering with the table or opponent. The judge of the contest, the local innkeeper, was grave. He tossed a coin, and picked the cooper as the man to go first. His opponent, the fletcher, grinned. Then the cooper made his move, and the fletcher's face sank.

What was the move?

Solution on page 250

Spot the
Difference

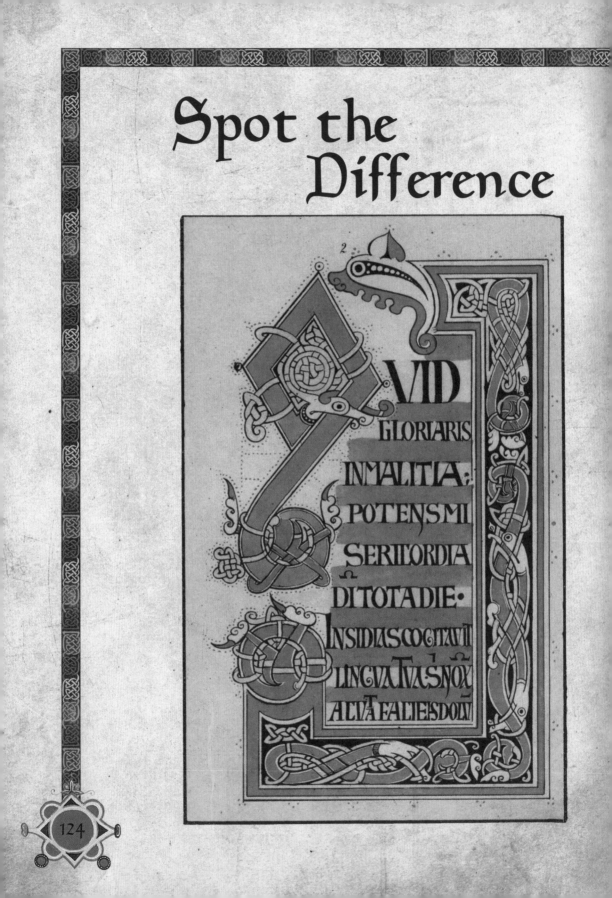

HERE are ten differences between these two pictures.
Can you find them all?

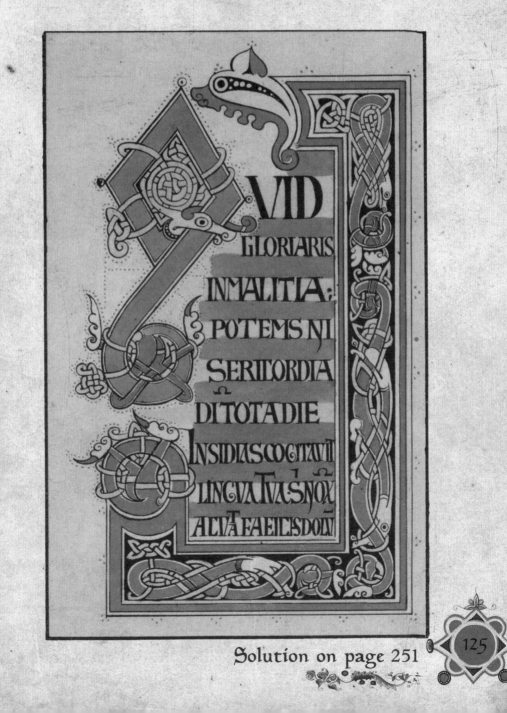

Solution on page 251

Affairs of the heart

A LADY of Seville had been suffering for some time with a troublesome sore throat, so she went to see a doctor. He asked her a few questions, told her to open her mouth, peered into her throat, and gasped. He immediately called out "Heart attack!" and rang his little emergency bell. His assistant came at once, ascertained the measure of the situation, and confirmed that it was indeed a heart attack – a near-fatal one at that, with a long recovery time assured. But the woman was back home the same evening, walking around without any trouble whatsoever.

What had happened?

Solution on page 252

Knight's Move

TWO crusaders, Blaise and Rickard, were tasked with patrolling a stretch of pilgrim trail through bandit-infested territory. They started one seven-day patrol 14 miles apart, both travelling from 6am to 6pm each day, in the same direction.

Blaise was getting a little old for patrol duty, and his stamina was poor. He started from the base. On the first day, his patrol took him 10 miles, but each day after that, as his strength waned, he went a mile less than the day before. By contrast, Rickard – who was ahead of Blaise at the start – was recovering from a nasty injury. The first day, he only managed to walk two miles, but each day after that he was able to walk another two miles further than he had the day before.

Where and when did the two crusaders meet along the road?

Solution on page 252

Bundle

TINA Bistis liked cooking with asparagus. At least once a week, she went to the market and bought a 10" bundle of it from Christos, whose farm was a couple of villages away from her own home. One morning, she discovered that Christos had sent one of his farm lads in his place. After assuring her that everything was fine back at the farm, the lad, Gianni, told her that he had tied the asparagus in smaller batches. He offered to give her two 5" bundles for the usual price, graciously adding that he wouldn't charge her for the extra string and paper.

 In whose favour is the deal?

Solution on page 252

Three Squared

N the foothills of the Hua Shan lay a small and ancient monastery that attracted some very curious speculation. One of its doorways opened onto a passage which led back into the hills themselves, eventually coming to a pond, constructed in a natural cave. A series of very narrow walkways ran over the pond's surface, and legend told that only those who had truly found their Tao were able to traverse the pattern that they made without walking the same stretch of beam twice.

Can you see a way?

129

A Merchant of Venice

THERE is a merchant who deals in only one specific item – an important part of daily life, without doubt. He stocks different varieties of this thing, but they all serve the same purpose. Some of the varieties contain as many as a million individual moving parts, while others may hold less than twenty – or, indeed, be totally solid throughout, yet still function as well as the most complex.

They range in size likewise, from the size of a thumbnail to something bigger and heavier than a man, but there is no reliable way to guess the complexity of the device from just its size.

What does the merchant deal in?

Solution on page 253

Several Brothers

ILL Johnson had twice as many sisters as he had brothers, while his sister, Mary, had the same number of brothers and sisters. Their neighbour, John Wilson, had three times as many sisters as brothers, but his sister, Barbara, like Mary Johnson, had the same number of brothers and sisters.

Assuming the fewest number of siblings in both cases, who had more brothers, Will Johnson or John Wilson?

Solution on page 254

The Captive Queen

As Ossory's fortunes fell, the Queen of Ossory found herself being held captive in one of her own high towers, with her daughter and her son. Outside the room was a roped pulley, baskets at each end, so designed that when one basket was on the ground, the other was by the window.

The Queen weighed 195lbs, while her daughter and son weighed 105lbs and 90lbs respectively. She also had a chest of valuables gleaned from the castle, which weighed 75lbs. Of course, getting into the basket while the other end was empty would be a fatal disaster, but the Queen had worked out that so long as the difference in weight between the two baskets was less than 16lbs, the drop would not be harmful to a person.

How did she escape with her children and treasure?

Solution on page 255

Weighting

A BEGINNING is a very sensitive time. The truth of this can quickly be demonstrated in construction. Make any mistakes in the way you set up a building's frame, and the entire thing might collapse. As a certain Scottish architect could attest, it remains vitally important to ensure that loads are properly balanced and that beams are evenly weighted.

This diagram crudely represents a series of interlinked beams and weights balanced around a pivot. The marked divisions are all the same length. The beam, rods and pivot point are rigid, and of negligible weight compared to the loads, which are given in hundredweight.

What value is required to balance the beam?

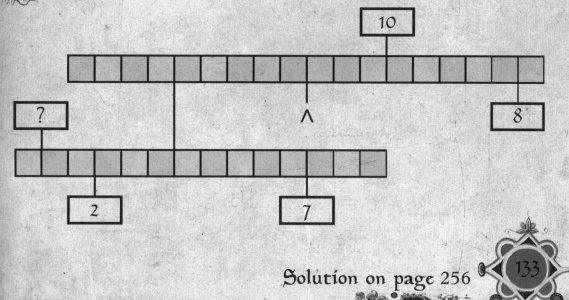

Cannon

 SOLDIER was looking glumly at several large crates of cannon balls. His sergeant insisted that he needed to know exactly how many balls there were, but the number wasn't marked on any of the crates.

Having measured the sturdy boxes several times, he knew that each one was 22.8" x 24.9" x 14". The shot balls were 2" in diameter, and each box was packed to maximum capacity.

Given that there were four crates, how many shot balls were there?

Solution on page 257

Hard Puzzles

Chicken

IN the Grünwald one afternoon, Otto was horrified to see his prize rooster dashing across the front yard and off into the woods. Bili had clipped wings, and the undergrowth was difficult for even a very motivated chicken to get through, but he was also extremely fast. Otto dropped his firewood and took off after him.

Bili had a ten-foot head start on Otto, and was running flat out, at 20mph. Otto could manage 12mph in a woodland sprint, but only for 60 seconds. After that, he would have to rest for several minutes. But Bili had to slow down steadily as he ran, from the exhaustion of having to fight through the bushes. So his speed dropped by 1mph every three seconds, to a minimum of 1mph.

 Did Otto catch the chicken?

Solution on page 259

Lovers

 ISCUSSING their personal histories, a courting couple discovered that their combined age was precisely 49. Furthermore, it transpired that back when the man was the same age that the woman is now, she was exactly half his age.

 How old are they now?

Solution on page 259

Rose Rows

 S it possible to plant nine roses in such a way as to end up with ten straight rows of three flowers?

 If so, how? If not, why?

Solution on page 260

The Scarves

 HE Pasha's daughters were skilled in weaving, and their scarves were a matter of near-legendary debate. Hadise, Selime and Aysul prided themselves on their talents, and were fiercely competitive as to whose work was superior. It was not just a matter of warmth, or lightness of the garment, or even how swiftly a scarf could be made, but rather a tangled question of all three.

Hadise could make five scarves in the same time that Selime made two, but while Hadise was making three scarves, Aysul would have made four. Just one of Hadise's scarves weighed as much as five of Aysul's, but three of Aysul's weighed as much as five of Selime's. Four of Aysul's scarves were required to get the same warmth as one of Selime's, but just one of Hadise's was as warm as three of Selime's.

Obviously, different people prized different things in a scarf. But if you were to give equal importance to rapidity, lightness and warmth, which sister would you judge to be the finest weaver?

Solution on page 261

Diced Doge

THE Doge of Venice was a whimsical man at times, so when one of his courtiers burst into Lorenzo's workshop carrying a small sack and calling for immediate attention, he was startled, but not entirely astonished. Lorenzo cleared some space on a bench, and watched as the courtier tipped out a generous pile of small wooden cubes. The two men stared at them for a little while.

Finally, the courtier coughed delicately. "How many different cubes could you paint from this pile?"

Lorenzo stared at the man.

"I mean to say, one cube is the same as another if you can rotate it so that its faces correspond exactly. If we establish that you use exactly six paints to colour a cube, and each face has to be monochrome, then there must be a limited number of different ways to do this. The Doge wishes to know how many. You may use these wooden blocks to experiment, if you like."

"This is not a job for an artist," Lorenzo said.

"The Doge disagrees," said the courtier.

 What is the answer?

Solution on page 262

The Garden of Winding Paths

 HE diagram below is a representation of the design of a lavish rose garden.

 Starting at the top, and walking always around the blue paths, is it possible to walk the entire garden without repeating your steps?

Solution on page 262

Carter

A PAIR of carters decided to have a challenge. They picked a much-frequented circuit around Westminster and Marylebone, and then one set off eastwards from the depot around it, while the other set off westwards.

Because of traffic, the easterly route took three hours, while the westerly route took two hours. If carts routinely set off every fifteen minutes in both directions, and the two carters were part of this schedule, which man saw more carts coming the other way, and by how many, before returning to the depot?

Solution on page 263

Fill In the Blanks

 N this puzzle, there are:

___ instance/s of the number 1

___ instance/s of the number 2

___ instance/s of the number 3

___ instance/s of the number 4

___ instance/s of the number 5

 Fill in the blanks correctly using standard decimal digits from one to nine so that each statement is correct.

Solution on page 263

Annual

ELECTING a year at random, is it possible to say that the probability of any given date falling on one particular day of the week must be exactly 1 in 7?

Solution on page 264

Matching Pairs

WO of the smaller pictures are mirror images of the larger picture. Which ones?

A B C D

E F G H

Solution on page 265

145

Toledo

THE diagram below is a rough reproduction of the ground plan of a large, airy home that was arranged around four lovely courtyards, with gardens interspersed between. The architect added certain mathematical features for the amusement of the owner's family, to be enjoyed by generations to come. The number in each courtyard is derived mathematically from the four numbers around the outside.

What number is missing from the fourth courtyard?

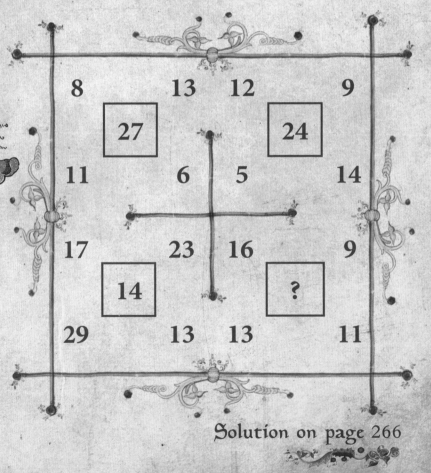

Solution on page 266

Mathic

T has long been known that a number exists with a very particular peculiarity. It divides an exact number of times into each number between 10,000,000 and 100,000,000 whose first four digits are identical to its second four digits. The digits of this peculiar number add up to ten.

Q *What is it?*

Solution on page 266

Rhys

N the Kingdom of Powys, a man known as Rhys the Red suffered a strange and terrible fate. He died on October 14th, and was buried two days earlier, on October 12th, of the same year.

How did this come to be?

Solution on page 267

Countering

COME, my friend. Let us play a game. If you win, I will buy your sheepskins for the price you wanted. Here are two bags. The first contains a single counter, which I swear to you now is either black or white. The second contains three counters, one white and two black. Good. Now, a white counter is added to the first bag. Look, now it is shaken. I draw one of the two counters back out, going with chance. It is white, see?

Now, tell me, which course of action gives you the better chance of retrieving a white counter – selecting one of the bags by nothing more than the toss of a coin and pulling a counter from it, or tipping the two bags together into one bag and pulling a counter from the combined bag?"

Solution on page 267

Square Magic

AGIC Squares have been an important part of mathematical and occult knowledge since the *'Lo Shu'* – the Scroll of the River Lo, was scribed in the 7th century BC. Also known as the Nine Halls Diagram, it is a key emblem of both Yi Jing Divination and Feng Shui geomancy, and it was said to have been important to the mighty Emperor Yu the Great. This square, shown below, is somewhat more complex. All the numbers from 1 to 49 appear in it exactly once, and every row, column and diagonal adds up to 175.

 Can you complete the square? If it is of any help, Agrippa considered this design to be sacred to Venus.

			41			
			17			
			49			
13	31	7	25	43	19	37
			1			
			33			
			9			

Solution on page 268

Players

SNORI and Rognald were so well matched at Hnefatafl that it was impossible to guess which of the men would win any one game. To make it more interesting, they decided to play a series of thirteen matches in the tavern one night, with a wager going to whichever man was the overall winner – ten small notches of silver.

Eight games in, Kol Snorisson dashed in to the tavern and, to everyone's annoyance, insisted that his father had to come home to sort out a family problem. Snori, who was leading 5-3, claimed that he should take the prize. Rognald wasn't having any of it. He insisted that the prize had to be split equally, as the series was undecided. Old Magnus, in the corner, suggested that there was an option which was fairer than either of those possibilities.

 What was it?

Solution on page 269

The Box

"**H**OW big is this box, Opa?"

"Lad, it depends on what you mean by 'big.' Its top is 120 square inches. The end is 80 square inches. The side is 96 square inches."

"But that doesn't tell me anything!"

"Ah, but it does. Tell me its length, width and height and I'll give you a biscuit."

 What are the box's dimensions?

Solution on page 270

The Cloth

DWARD turned to his brother Thomas with a cheerful grin, and waved one of his mother's wash-cloths at him. "Wanna make a bet?"

Thomas peered at him suspiciously. "What bet?"

"I'll put this down on the floor, and if we stand on opposite corners, facing each other, I bet we can't shake hands."

"You're going to keep your hands behind your back, or give me a dead arm or something," said Thomas.

"No, nothing like that," said Edward. "If I'm not stopping us from shaking hands, you win."

Thomas thought about it furiously, but he couldn't work out what the trick was. He took the bet – and lost.

 How did Edward win?

Solution on page 271

Matching Pairs

ONLY one of the smaller pictures is the same as the large one on the left. Which one?

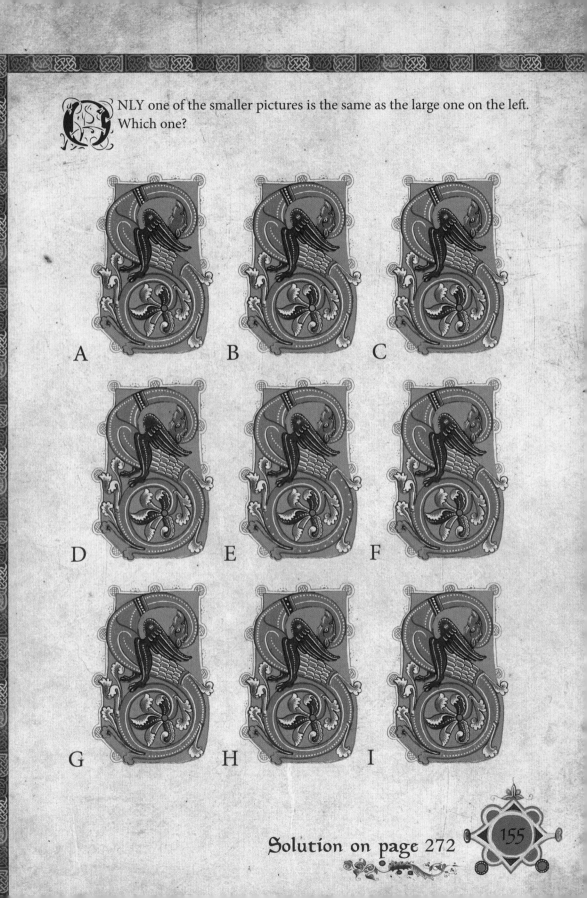

A

B

C

D

E

F

G

H

I

Solution on page 272

The Mysts of history

AFTER the Knights Templar fled from France and disappeared into the ranks of Freemasonry in Scotland and England, the French King, Philip the Fair, was left with little more than a few old men to torment, including the Order's Grand Master, Jacques de Molay.

As he burnt at the stake, de Molay pronounced a dire doom on Philip and his pet Pope, declaring that they would be dead within the year – and in fact, that was what happened. Philip never did receive the huge payout he had been hoping for when he betrayed the Templars. The legendary treasure of the Order vanished into obscurity, as did its entire fleet. Part of the success of this escape was undoubtedly due to careful use of codes on the Templars' part.

Can you translate the coded mathematical operations and find the missing number?

Solution on page 273

Oily

ATE one Saturday, as the day was drawing to a close, Max discovered that he had run out of oil for his lamp. His neighbours, Dieter and Nils, offered to help. Dieter had eight pints of oil, and Nils had five. The two men combined their supplies and then divided the oil into thirds, so each man had four and one third pints of oil. Max gratefully gave the men 13 copper pfennigs, and went home to fill up his lamps.

Q *How should the money be divided?*

Solution on page 273

Dominicans

A GROUP of friars had come from all across Spain to gather in Zaragoza for an important series of meetings. It was decided that as a collective demonstration of piety, one of their number should spend the entire first night, from sunset to sunrise, in prayer to San Dominguito del Val.

Which of the twenty-two friars performed the penance would be left in the lap of God. One of the assistants was selected, and told that at sunset, the men would gather in a circle. He was to move around the circle repeatedly, releasing every seventh friar, until only one remained. The assistant was not fond of his master, a cruel disciplinarian, and decided to ensure that he would be the one selected for the task.

Where should the assistant start to ensure that his master is selected?

Solution on page 274

Rupert's Square

OU are given a square piece of wood, 12" to a side.

Is it possible to divide it into two identical pieces which can be fitted together to form a rectangle 9" by 16" in size?

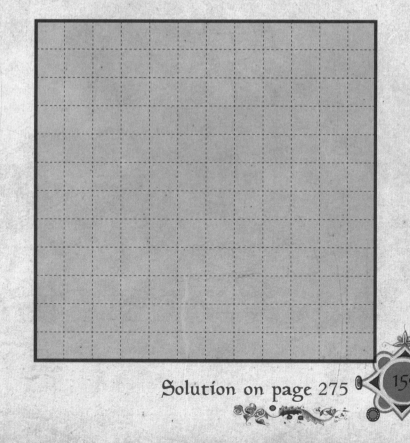

Solution on page 275

Al hazrad

UARDS arrived at a market square in Damascus to find that a notorious desert wanderer had been ripped to pieces. The man was a self-proclaimed sage and prophet of unhallowed powers, and there were those who whispered that he had been slain by Jinn for revealing forbidden secrets. However, the guards had a less fanciful turn of mind, and rounded up five suspects, all men with unfortunate reputations who had been in the square at the time. Each man gave a statement, two of which were untrue.

Hamza: Rasul is the killer. He is a vicious dog.

Rasul: Hamza blames me unjustly, for he is still angry about that thing with his sister.

Alim: Poor Munir! Why do you cast your eye on him? He is not responsible.

Munir: My dear friend Jamal is completely honest.

Jamal: I have never killed any man, woman or child. I would not do such a thing.

 Logically, who was the killer?

Very Nice

A TUTOR to the nobility in the city of Nice was in the habit of setting one particular mathematical conundrum to his pupils when he felt that they had learned enough of numbers. If they were able to answer correctly in a reasonable amount of time, he would move on to other subjects. If not, then the sums would continue.

Using the digits 1-9 exactly once each, assemble a mathematically correct addition of the form $a + b = c$. You may use vulgar fractions if desired.

 What is the answer?

Solution on page 276

Curious By Design

 HIS glyph, like others of its kind, was found on a scrap of stone, in a quiet corner of a very old forest.

 What number should be in the centre?

8

78   16

?

4   14

2

Solution on page 277

Black Robb

HEN Angus the potter called on Black Robb to deliver some clay mugs that he had made for him, he discovered Robb's savage wolfhound, Campbell, tied to a stake in front of the house on a thirty foot rope. Angus decided he would leave the pots as close to the house as possible to avoid being mauled by Campbell, but when the dog started barking ferociously he set them down 45 feet from the house.

He was not a timid man, so why do you think he made that decision?

Solution on page 277

163

Dice

AURIZIO and Tiziano had a game that they enjoyed playing in the tavern, to decide who would pay the bill. The rules were that each man selected two odd numbers between 3 and 17. Each of the numbers had to be different. They then took it in turns to throw three regular dice. The first player who rolled dice totalling one of his numbers would win, although the other player was allowed one roll afterwards to try to match a number of his own, for a draw.

Number selection obviously greatly impacts on the chances of winning, but is it possible to find two pairs of numbers which gives both players the same chance of victory?

If so, what are they?

Solution on page 278

Mathematical Masonry

 HE tombstone of a celebrated stonemason in Madrid was decorated with an odd pattern, as per very specific instructions in his will. His grave became something of a pilgrimage for some of the city's more curious-minded folk.

 What glyph is required to complete the design?

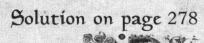

Spot the Difference

THERE are ten differences between these two pictures.
Can you find them all?

Savvy

THERE is a single counterfeit Darahim in a stack of nine coins. It is indistinguishable to the eye or hand, but a perfectly-balanced scale will show you that it is ever so slightly lighter than it should be.

 What is the least number of times that you must weigh the coins in order to detect the bad coin?

Solution on page 280

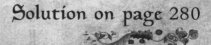

Loafing

AT Marmoutier Abbey, Alcuin the Abbot paid his cooks their daily wages in bread that they could then resell, according to their relative ranks. The five cooks were allocated 100 loaves to divide among themselves, with the highest-ranking receiving the most, and the lowest-ranking the least.

The difference between each cook's allowance and that of the next cook down remained constant. Each cook received at least some bread.

 If the two smallest allocations combined were just one seventh of the three larger shares, then what was the gap between adjacent shares?

Solution on page 281

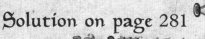

The Urchin

 CERTAIN young street scamp was given to describing his age in colourful terms. According to the boy, when he was born the apple-seller's assistant, Daisy, was just a quarter of the age of the butcher, Tony. Now Daisy is a third of the age of Gary, the chicken man, while the boy is a quarter of Tony the butcher's age. In four more years however, he'll be a quarter of Gary's age at that time.

How old is the boy?

Solution on page 282

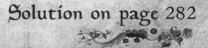

Scales

HE diagram below represents several sets of weighing scales, forever close to the heart of all those who are interested in matters mercantile. Each of the scales is exactly balanced so that the weight of one side is equal to the weight of the other, just as if they would be if they were at rest.

 Taking the smallest whole-unit values, what does each symbol weigh?

$$\odot \; \mathrm{D} \quad = \quad \text{♀ ♀ ♀}$$

$$\text{♀ ♂ ♀} \quad = \quad \mathrm{D}$$

$$\mathrm{D} \; \text{♂ ♀} \quad = \quad \odot \; \text{♀ ♃} \; \odot$$

$$\text{♂ ♂} \quad = \quad \odot$$

$$\odot \; \mathrm{D} \; \text{♃ ♀} \quad = \quad \text{♂ ♀ ♀ ♀ ♀ ♀ ♂}$$

$$\text{♀} \; \odot \; \odot \; \text{♀} \quad = \quad \text{♃ ♀}$$

Solution on page 283

Docking

T was whispered in the village of Docking, that Tobias was both uncle and nephew to Harry at the same time, just as Harry in turn was both uncle and nephew to Tobias. A rum state of affairs to be sure.

 Can you say how it came to be?

Solution on page 284

Quadruped

 IN the great market of Buda, three men were discussing the possibility of buying an exotic-looking beast. The price was a princely 24 half-pfennigs, but not one of them could afford it without a loan from their friends.

The first pointed out that if he borrowed half of the money the other two held, he would have enough. The second said that if he borrowed two thirds of the other two's cash, he would be able to buy the beast and have a third of a pfennig left over. The third countered that if he borrowed three quarters of the money held by the first two, he would have three quarters of a pfennig left over after buying the animal.

How much did each man have?

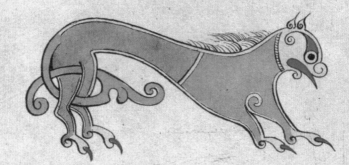

Solution on page 285

Triptych

A CERTAIN Flemish painter liked to hide odd glyphs and tables of uncertain meaning into his works. He was habitually tight-lipped regarding the symbolism of his actions, but took it very seriously. The odd arrangement below was painted as if chiselled into a cliff face.

What is the value of each symbol?

	202	194	180	180	
238	☉☽	☉♂	☿☉	☿☽	238
248	♀♀	♀☉	☽♀	♀☉	248
270	♂♂	♂☽	♀♀	☉♂	270
	202	194	180	180	

Solution on page 286

Cellar

MATO handed Ernesto a heavy package, along with a pair of wax-dipped strings. "In exactly 45 minutes, open the package. You'll know what you have to do. Do not delay! The timing must be precise."

"There is no clock down here," Ernesto complained.

"The strings will each burn for an hour precisely," Amato said, "take care not to cut or bend them or their timekeeping will be ruined."

"Understood," said Ernesto. Amato nodded, and vanished back up the stairs.

 How is Ernesto going to measure exactly 45 minutes, if he cannot tell the three-quarter mark of one of his crude candles?

Solution on page 286

Barras

THE Cloughs and the Allsops lived next door to each other, and although they didn't get on very well, they had a surprising amount in common. Both families consisted of a father, a mother, a son and a daughter. In both families, their ages combined totalled 100. In fact, in both families, if you added the squares of the mother's, daughter's and son's ages together, you would arrive at the square of the father's age.

However, Miss Clough was a year older than her brother, while Miss Allsop was two years older than her own brother.

What are all of their ages?

Solution on page 287

The Dordonnese Way

SEVERAL encoded equations relating to a long, bloody history of conflict are shown below. Certain numbers have been consistently replaced with tokens. The answers given are correct, but be warned that the mathematical operations have to be performed in the order they are given – in other words, $1 + 2 \times 3$ would be 9, not 7.

What are the numbers?

$$☿ \times ☉ \times ☽ \times ♀ = 199920$$

$$☉ + ☽ + ☿ + ♀ = 92$$

$$☽ - ☉ + ♀ - ☿ = 2$$

$$♀ \times ☽ / ☉ + ☿ = 32$$

$$(☿ - ☽) \times (♀ - ☉) = 35$$

Solution on page 287

Simple Solutions

Barcelona

Just one man. The family tree is knotty, and assumes marriage between cousins is not forbidden, but it is possible.

Wise Man's Bluff

16 Wise Men in total. According to the prophecy, you need seven who are blind, and nine that see with one eye. But there is no requirement that one eye precludes the other, so the two who are blind in one eye and the four that see with both eyes can both be included among that initial nine.

Alcuin

The sacks weigh 5.5 lbs, 6.5 lbs, 7 lbs, 4.5 lbs and 3.5 lbs respectively. Considered together, each of the sacks is weighed twice, except '3', which is weighed three times. Add all the totals together, and subtract twice the weight of '1' and '2' combined, and also twice the weight of '4' and '5' combined, and you'll get 21, which is three times the weight of '3'. From there, you can substitute easily to find the values.

Three Boatmen

If just one man is telling the truth and the other two are lying, Cipolla has to be the honest man.

Beam

The unknown load is twice as far from the balance point as the known one, so must be half its weight – 7 hundredweight.

Equity

3 + 1.5 = 3 × 1.5 = 4.5

SIMPLE

Roll Out

Tip the barrel on its side just until the liquid inside touches the rim, and then look in. If the bottom of the barrel is visible at all, then it is more than half empty. If any of the barrel's side is hidden, it is more than half full. If the liquid reaches the join exactly, then it is precisely at the half-way mark.

Idiot

The 'idiot' knew perfectly well that as soon as he took the more valuable coin, people would lose interest and stop giving him money!

Riddle-Me-Ree

An echo.

Spot the Difference

DNI
ASCENSIO
MA
RIA
VIRI
GALILEI

SIMPLE

A Serious Meal

Each man was given three pieces, namely a third, a fifth and a fifteenth of a loaf. Divide one loaf into five chunks, and the other two into thirds (for six thirds). Chop one of those thirds into five smaller pieces. You then have five thirds, five fifths and five fifteenths to give to the men..

The Mason of Madrid

If you count the stars up and treat them as four-digit numbers, you will see that they are a mathematical sum: 2615 + 4527 = 7142. So the missing glyph is:

Smelly Water

No. Since the amount that the fluid rises halves each time, it will in fact never quite get past twice its original displacement.

Birthday Boy

It is January 1st, and Kurt's birthday is New Year's Eve. Two days ago, he was 34. Yesterday, he turned 35. Today is a new year, at the end of which Kurt will be 36. Next year, he'll become 37.

A Bed of Roses

Looking Ahead

Yes (and yes). If Ahmed has hair, then Ibrahim is a bald man who is looking at him. If Ahmed is himself bald, then he is looking at Sayeed, who is not. Either way, there is a bald man looking at a man with hair.

The Ox

The answer is 1125bu per kè. You don't know how long the journey is, but it doesn't matter, since it is the same distance both ways. It is tempting to assume that the average overall speed will be exactly midway between the two speeds, but since you spend a longer time travelling at the lower speed, it gets dragged down slightly. Imagine, for example, that the distance is 4500 bu. Then it will take 5 kè to get there, and 3 to get back. Adding the speeds and averaging, we get $((3x1500)+(5x900))/8 = 9000/8 = 1125$.

Now try it with a distance twice as far, which will take twice as long. $((6x1500)+(10x900))/16 = 18000/16 = 1125$, again. The average remains the same.

Illumination

$\odot = 5.\ \mathcal{D} = 4.\ \yen = 6.$

The Bag

The second bag is more likely to hold a pearl. The first bag has a flat 50% chance of holding a pearl or a bead. The second bag has a 66.6% chance of holding a pearl.

When the known pearl goes in, we know it holds two stones, either Pearl 1 (P1) and Pearl 2 (P2), or the second pearl (B). That gives us four possible ways that the jeweller could draw two stones from it: P1 then P2; P2 then P1; P2 then B; or B then P2. We already know that he didn't draw B first, so that last case is ruled out. That leaves three possibilities, two of which involve drawing a second pearl.

In the Village

The man is Hob's uncle.

Magic Square

11	24	**7**	20	3
4	12	**25**	8	16
17	5	**13**	**21**	**9**
10	18	**1**	14	22
23	6	**19**	2	15

Matching Pairs

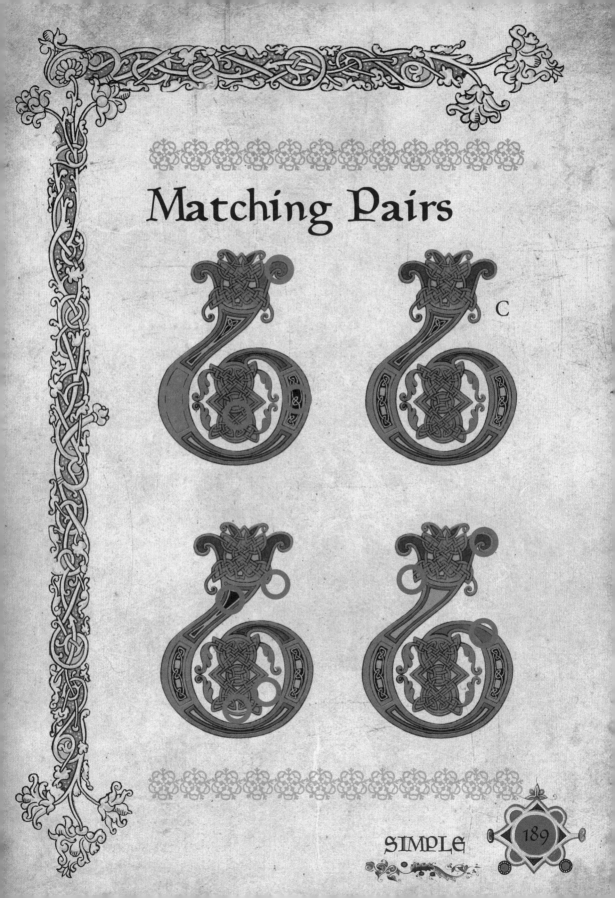

C

The Blacksmith

It will take José 360 strides to catch the thief.
For each 15 of José's strides, the thief takes 9 x 3=27
of his own steps. Those same 15 strides are worth
5.5 x 5 = 27.5 of the thief's steps. So each 15 of José's
strides closes the gap by half of a step. The gap is
12 steps, so it will take 24 of these 15-stride periods –
24 ×15 = 360.

SIMPLE

May and June

They had at least one more sister from the same birth – specifically, in this instance, April, the eldest of the three triplets, who lived in London.

Firenze

It is 13.125 feet tall. (7/4) gives the ratio of height to shadow, ×7.5 for the tree's shadow =13.125ft.

The Templar Code

The missing value is 75.
186 × 68 = 12648. 12648 + 12048 = 24696.
Similarly, 258 × 75 = 19350. 19350 + 14886 = 34236.

SIMPLE

One hump

They are 45 and 54. The ages have to be close together to keep the differential down to 1/11th of the total, which implies a 9-year age gap, and thus a total of 99 years.

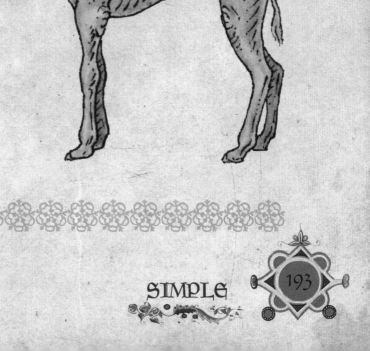

Planking

Sawing wood consumes a certain amount of the raw material. After having sawn through the plank seven times in the process of dividing it, each section will now weigh a little less than a pound.

SIMPLE

Mine

Your name.

Good Morning

4 tutors. People do not bow to themselves, but the headmaster doesn't bow to anyone, so 1296 bows means 36 people bowing. One ninth of those are tutors.

Sour Milk

2pm. Midway between 4am and 4pm is 10am. 2pm is four hours after that.

Matching Pairs

D

A Curious Design

32. Opposing pairs of numbers are added to make the number in the middle.

Marek

A third. He was outside from the halfway mark to the point where he had half as far to go as he'd already travelled out there – in other words, if he had one part left to go, he would have been outside for two parts. So he was outside for two thirds of the second half of the trip.

SIMPLE

Needle's Eye

The piece of cloth was a holy relic. Possessing it would help raise the profile of the abbey, and its income along with it.

Premium Brandy

Just 25%. He is diluting the brandy by 50% in the first step, and then diluting that mix by 50% again in the second step.

The Count

The window was rebuilt as a square diamond. That way it was able to stay five feet wide and high, and to remain square, but to only let in half as much light. In the original form, the window is 5x5 = 25 sq ft in area. As a diamond, 5ft is the length of the diagonal across the square. From Pythagoras' theorem, this means that the length of the diamond's sides is 3.535 feet, which gives an area of 12.5 sq ft.

Hundred Years

BBI. Add the three four-digit numbers together on each table. Each of the last three digits of this sum – 173, 997 and 229 respectively – are then converted to letters that have that number's position in the alphabet. So 1 becomes A, 2 becomes B, and so on.

SIMPLE

Cacciatore

75 feet. If the hare starts at 50ft distant and ends up at 0ft, then 30ft comes when there is still 3/5 of the chase left. 3/5 of 125 is 75.

Infamy, Infamy

18. The difference between ⅔ and ½ is ⅙. The woman and her two regular friends make up that difference. If 3 people are ⅙ of the group, then the group is 3x6 = 18 people.

Moderate Solutions

Three Jailers

Yes. If Bernt was on duty, Matthias could go off-duty.

Rose Lines

Arrange the flowers into a five-pointed star shape, like this:

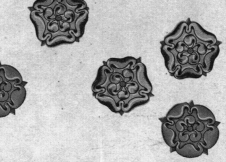

The Calipha's Garden

88 x 88.5 yards. The length of the path in yards is equal to the area of the garden. Although the length and width are uneven, taking the square root of the area (88.249...) will give you an estimate of the value mid-way between them. You know the difference is 0.5 yards, so it is easy to check that 88 and 88.5 are the correct values.

MODERATE

The Pigs

10 pigs, receiving 29 tokens. All the different breakdowns can be stacked together, so two pigs received 3 'not so good', three pigs received 2 'not so good' and 1 'good' token, one pig receives 1 'not so good' and 1 'good' token, three pigs receive 1 'not so good' and 2 'good' tokens, and one pig receives 3 'good' tokens.

Three Squares

Try thinking of the design as several irregular pieces, as below, and it becomes far more straightforward

Start at the top left (1), and follow the outside edge (2), (3) round to the bottom left (4). At the junction immediately above (4), turn right and trace the inside of the bottom right-angled section to (5), and then come back down to the same junction (4) by tracing the lower edge of the three little squares. Go round to the next junction (6), and make the loop of the edges of three little squares and the big right-angled piece via (7). Finally, complete the loop by coming back to (1).

MODERATE

The Top of the hill

144,806.
There are 187 × (4×39 + 1) = 29359 cavalry,
207 × (3×186 + 2) = 115920.
115920+29359-473 = 114806.

Quite Contrary

5. Twice as many again would mean 3x their present
number, and for that to fall evenly either side of ten,
it has to be 5x3=15.

Reales

*528 reales. 27×4=108. Just under a fifth is 21
and just under half of that is 10.
So 21×3 + 10×8 + (108-31) ×5
= 63+80+385 = 528 reales – or 66 'Pieces of Eight'.
Not that Maria's father was a pirate...*

MODERATE

Potato Farming

10100 yards. It would mean walking 1 yard there and back, then 2 yards, and so on. To quickly total 1 to 100, consider that it breaks down to 50 pairs of numbers each adding up to 101. 50 ×101 = 5050. But the planter has to walk there and back, so it is twice as far.

Spot the Difference

MODERATE

Black or White

Yes; it increases the chance to ⁷⁄₁₂ from ½. The chance of drawing a third white out of a bag you know nothing about is 50%, as you would expect. If you know that there is at least one white counter in the bag, then there are only four possible initial states for the bag – (W)WWW, (W)WWB, (W)WBB or (W)BBB. The fifth option, BBBB, is impossible. If we know nothing about the bag, we must assume the counters are selected randomly, which makes WWBB the most likely original state, and WBBB as likely as WWWB. When we know the fifth option is impossible however, (W)WWB and (W)WBB become equally likely original states, which pushes up the chance a little of drawing a third white counter.

The Mathematical Mason

If you count the stars and treat them as four-digit numbers, you will see that they are a mathematical sum: 4376 + 5007 = 9383. So the missing glyph is

★★★

Balance

10.25 hundredweight.
On one side, you have 4×9 + 5×6 = 66. Take away
7×3 = 21 from that on the other side, and you are
left needing 45/4 = 10.25 to achieve balance.

The Ale Yard

In fact, the jug is 2.93 gallons in size. It has to be larger
than the 2.5 gallons one might expect in order to allow
for the fact that the second jug is no longer pure beer.
  10-2.93=7.07 gallons of beer in the keg after one
draft. The next draft will hold only 70.7% percent beer,
and 70.7% of 2.93 means the second drawing removes
2.07 gallons of beer. 2.93+2.07 is 5 gallons, for 50%.

MODERATE

In Norfolk

Mears was a widower. After his first wife died, he married her sister. His death left his second wife a widow, meaning that his first wife became his widow's sister.

Bucket List

The water that is displaced reflects the mass of the floating object. A certain percentage of the smaller bucket is still sticking up above the water, which adds to the mass. If the whole of the smaller bucket were suddenly transformed into as much water as required to provide the same weight, it would completely fill the space that the smaller bucket had occupied (up to the water line).

MODERATE

The hunter's Spears

Rotate the 9 and the 8 around their centre-point until they are in each other's spots, but the 9 is upside-down, and thus turned into a 6. Then both columns will add to 18.

Ivan the Rather Unpleasant

9.36pm. A quarter of 9h 36m is 2h 24m, and half the time to the next noon, 14h and 24m away, is 7h and 12m. 2h24+7h12=9h36.

Spot the Difference

216

MODERATE

The Battle
Of Grunwald

Five. Total the number of injuries. The amount over 300 (representing the hundred men each having three injuries distributed amongst themselves) is the minimum number who have all four. 64+62+92+87=305.

Operators

123 - 46 - 67 + 89 = 100.

Cassie

Cassie is a horse.

Monkey Puzzle

Whatever the monkey does on the rope, the weight will match her position. If she climbs up or down, it will rise or fall with her. If she lets go and drops, so will the weight. So they will reach the top at the same time.

Always

The sum is 9567+1085=10652.

MODERATE

Alhambra

11:30 am. The route is the same both ways, so on the flat, a mile there and back takes ¼ + ¼ = half an hour. On the hill, a mile there and back takes ⅓ + ⅙ = again, half an hour. The journey takes 6 hours, so it is 12 miles there and 12 miles back. We cannot tell the delivery time precisely, but if the journey was all flat, 12 miles at 4mph would take three hours.
If it was all hill, 12 miles at 3mph would take four hours. So 3.5 hours is definitely within half an hour of the delivery time. 8+3.5 = 11.5.

Meissen

9, 81, 324 and 576 are the four square numbers that together use the digits 1-9 once.

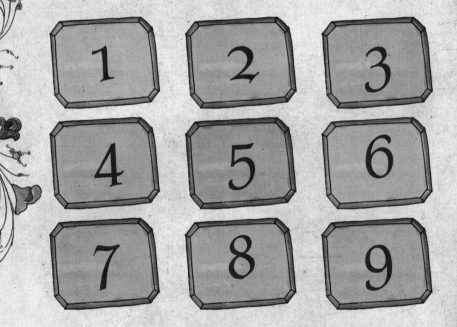

Old Tom

44. His age +6 is equal to 5/4th of (age - 4),
or 5×(age - 4) /4. Multiply out by 4 to get rid of
that divisor, and 4 × age + 24 = 5×(age - 4),
or 5 × age - 20. Add the 20 to both sides,
and 4 × age + 44 = 5 × age, or 44 = Old Tom's age.

Scaling

☉=1. ☽=3. ☿=4. ♃=7.

The heist

The men were enforcing the law, not behaving criminally. In this instance, they were revenue agents for the crown. The merchant was smuggling the spirits, and the agents raided his premises to confiscate the contraband and obtain proof of his perfidy.

The Courier

He should pick up the signpost and point it so that the sign to Briccolino is pointing the way that he had just come. Then all of the other indicators will also be pointing in the correct direction.

MODERATE

Matching Pairs

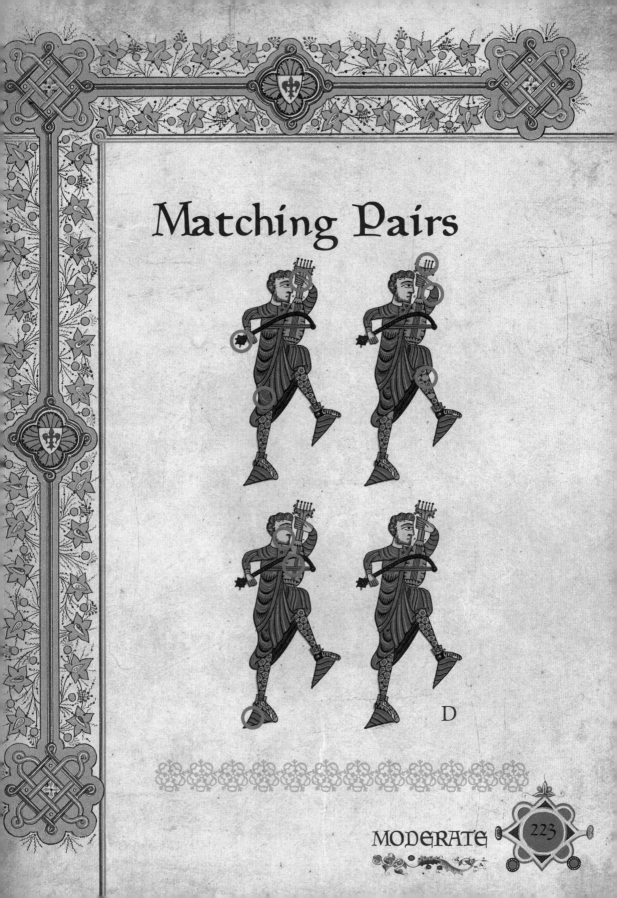

D

The Moneylender

A fourth is one third as as big as three fourths." with "of three fourths. So four fourths is 1 and 1/3 the size of three fourths -- or one third larger.

For the Cheese

25 miles. Draw a horizontal line from Gouda to the North-South road and call the point where it intersects 'A'. Then we have two right-angled triangles, one Mijdrecht-Gouda-A, and the other Schoonhoven-Gouda-A. We know that the hypotenuses of these two triangles added together total 35, and that the length of Gouda-A is 12.

There are only three possible right-angled triangles with a side length of 12, and those have hypotenuses of 13, 15 and 20. 15 + 20 = 35. Those two triangles have sides of 9-12-15 and 16 -12 - 20, so the direct distance is 9 +16 = 25.

The heralds

This is a trick question of course. When the two knights meet, they will be the same distance from Lincoln.

Witchcraft

♌			♍			♉	
				♍			
		♋		♋			♌
		♊		♊			♈
	♊		♋	♋	♈		♈
♊	♈		♉		♍	♍	
					♌		♌
			♉	♉			

Saintly

24.
Fifteen children means 14 age gaps, so 21 years.
The youngest is 3, the oldest is 24.

Diptych

$\odot$=4. $\mathbb{D}$=2. $\m(Astronomical symbol)$=5. $\mars$=7.

MODERATE

It's a Trap

6.25 minutes. The trap he meets at 12.5 minutes has 2.5 minutes to reach its destination and start back, so is travelling 12.5/2.5 = 5 times faster than he is. Now consider the total distance the man has to travel from when he initially starts walking, to when he overtaken, as x, and the distance the trap has to travel in the exact same time $x + y$, where y is the inbound 15-minute journey. Given the speed ratio, $x + y = 5 \times x$, or $y = 4x$, and $x = y/4$. We know that y takes 15 minutes, so x — the extra distance on top of a whole journey before the coach overtakes him — takes 15/4, or 3.75 minutes.

Therefore both coach and man have been travelling for a total 15 + 3.75 minutes = 18.75 minutes when the coach overtakes him. It originally passed him after 12.5 minutes, so the extra time required is 18.75 - 12.5 = 6.25 minutes.

The Courtyards

8+1+5-4 = 10.

TRICKY SOLUTIONS

Shares

1.5625 and 0.4375. There are 10 novices, and since the difference in share from smallest to largest runs x, $x+1/8$, $x+2/8$ then there are 45 1/8 shares making up the total differential. So that means that $10x+(45/8) = 10$, thus $10x = 10-5.625$, or $x = 0.4375$. So the smallest share is 7/16 (0.4375) of a portion. The largest share = the smallest + 9/8, which makes it 1 and 9/16 (1.5625) of a portion.

The Woodcutter's Sons

15, 18 and 21. Two of the ages will always equal double the third. Consider $a + c = b + b$; add a variable for time to both sides $a+t + c+t = b+t + b+t$ and it cancels out, so time is not a factor. $a + c = 2b$ is always true. Now, going back to the instance when two of their ages equals the third, we can describe their ages as x, y, and $(x + y)$. At the same time, $a + c = 2b$ has to hold true. There's no way (after they're born) that $x + y = 2(x + y)$, so $x + (x + y)$ must $= 2y$. (We don't know which age x is, so it doesn't matter that we picked that instead of y). That means $2x+y = 2y$, or $y = 2x$ so, in the first instance, we can write their ages as x, $2x$ and $(x+2x)$, or $3x$. The total of all those is $6x$, and we know that it has been 2/3 of that time since then, so it's been $4x$ more years. The ages of the sons are therefore now $5x$, $6x$ and $7x$, and that's an integer, because it's the 21st birthday of one of them. 21 is divisible by 7 and not by 5 or 6, so the sons are now 15, 18 and 21. When they were 3, 6, and 9, which was 12 years ago, the two younger equalled the oldest; all through their lives, the oldest and youngest sons ages will equal twice the middle sons.

232

The Quad

The students at Number 9. The answer lies in applying Pythagoras' theorem. Each of the rooms is on a different side, so the shortest distance between doors in each case is going to be the hypotenuse of a right-angled triangle. If we call the four doorways, in order, A, B, C and D, then A has 11 to its right and B has 5 to its left, so the distance AB is the square root of $12^2 + 5^2 = (144+25)$, or $\sqrt{169}$, or 13. Similarly AC = 21 (directly opposite), AD=12.04, BC=20, BD=21.21 (straight across then 3 down) and CD=15.81. A (AB+AC+AD) = 46.04; B (AB+BC+BD) = 54.21; C (AC+BC+CD) = 56.81; and D (AD+BD+CD) = 49.06. A wins.

TRICKY

6
6 2 5
6 4
2 2 5
3 4
3 5 3 6
4

Digimancy

The number is 142857, 1/7th of 999999.
The six-digit length and the six multipliers
(you remembered x1, right?) are indicators
that it is derived from a fraction of 7.

6 2 5
6 4
2 5
2 3 4
5 3 6
3 3
4

TRICKY

The Maze

Come out of the bottom left exit of the diamond, then, in order, turn left, right, right and left.

Nuremberg

66. The number of pairs of swapped positions from any whole hour to midnight can be calculated as follows: subtract the start time from midnight, and then subtract 1. Then sum all the positive integers up to (and including) the result.

So for one whole clock-face, calculate from midday to midnight: 24-12 = 12, then -1 = 11. 1+2+3+4+5+6+7+8+9+10+11= 66.

TRICKY

The Templar Treasure

100" square, and 11" tall. The gold is arranged flat, eight slabs by nine, leaving a 1" gap at the edge. Eleven layers reach to the top, taking 792 slabs. The remaining eight fit on their edge in the 1" gap, lengthways. Please note that such a crate of gold would weigh a little over 38 tons!

The Keg

First of all, fill the bucket, and then fill the jar from the bucket. That leaves 7 pints in the keg, 2 in the bucket, and 3 in the jar. The hauler cheerfully quaffs the beer in the bucket, emptying it. The beer in the jar is poured back into the bucket, and the jar is filled from the keg. This leaves four pints in the keg, three pints in both bucket and jar, and two pints in the hauler. The cooper claims the keg as his entire share, and starts catching up with the hauler. Filling the bucket from the jar leaves one pint in the jar, which the carter drinks. Finally, the jar is filled back up from the bucket, so now the jar holds three pints, for the carter, the bucket and two pints, for the hauler.

TRICKY

The Prisoner

He reached his highest spot, 4.43 yards up, after 7 bursts of effort. Given that his distance diminishes, he climbs 2y, then 1.8y, 1.62y, 1.46y, 1.31y, 1.18y, 1.06y and, on the eighth try, 0.96y. In each case, his net distance is -1y, so at the end of the seventh climb, he is at his peak:
1+0.8+0.62+0.46+0.31+0.18+1.06 = 4.43.

Trouble in France

11.
The calculation is 856 × 11
= 9416 + 54163 = 63579

Shadows

B

TRICKY

Dealing

No. If it seems to good to be true, then it usually is. The scam is as old as trade itself – one partner buys an unlikely item and talks up the value of its mythical double, then the other partner sells the item back for far more than the first one paid, leaving the dealer out of pocket. The best response is both safer and fairer – offer half of the money (fifty darahim in this case) when the potential purchaser actually pays. If it is legitimate, all parties should be happy; if they are not, then it is a scam.

Leonardo's Balls

9ft. In the instant before impact, both balls are travelling at the same speed, x, because of gravity. The heavy ball hits and its speed is reflected back upwards, -x. The light ball is now travelling at (x - -x = 2x) relative to the heavy ball, and this speed in turn is reflected, so that it is now travelling at -2x relative to the heavy ball. This translates to -3x relative to the ground – it is rising three times as fast as it fell. Kinetic energy is ½ × mass × speed squared, so however much energy was involved in gravity pulling it down a foot, there is now nine times that much energy pushing it back up. That means it will rise nine times as high as it was originally dropped.

In real trials, it won't be this much, as we don't have any perfectly elastic balls or perfectly rigid floors, but it's still impressive!

TRICKY

Alice

Alice is 16.5yrs old (and Tom is 27.5).

We have two absolute ages, Tom now, at the start of the description (T) and Alice back then, at the end of the description (A). We also don't know how many years older Tom is than Alice, so we'll call it 'x'.

First, reduce the complex description to an equation: $T / 2 + x = 1/2 \times 3 \times 3 \times A$. Multiply that by 2, and we have $T + 2x = 9A$, which means Tom now + twice their age gap is equal to nine times Alice then. But we know that when Alice was 'then', Tom was three times her age, so their gap was (and always is) twice her age 'then'; or $x = 2A$. Substitute that, and we have $T + 4A = 9A$, or $T = 5A$. Tom is five times as old now as Alice was when he was 3 times as old as her, and since the gap is 2A, Alice's age now is $5A-2A = 3A$. So the current ratio of their ages is 5:3. We know the total is 44, so $5A + 3A = 44$. That means $A = 44/8 = 5.5$, the age of Alice then. So Tom now, 'T' is 5.5×5=27.5, and Alice's age now is 5.5×3 = 16.5.

Rum Business

Neither. Four ladles go in each direction, so we end up with a quart of both mixtures. Whatever the rum has gained in wine is exactly whatever the wine has gained in rum, or else the amounts of liquid would differ.

Grand Designs

27. Clockwise from top, add, multiply or subtract numbers in opposite pairs to arrive at the answer.

TRICKY

Crossed Lines

3.86 ells.

Embroidery

They are descended in a straight line.
Georgina is Honor's mother.
Honor is Elena's mother.
And Elena is Ana's mother.

It's Time

6:28 (and a little). Break it down. $3x+55 = 150$. $3x = 95$. $X = 31.66$; so it is almost 32 minutes before 7pm.

Century

AFF. Add the twelve single-digit numbers together on each table, which total 62, 71 and 55 respectively. The digits of these totals are then converted to letters, starting at A = 0. So 1 becomes B, 2 becomes C, and so on, and 055 becomes AFF.

Run, Rabbit

He climbed into the prison, to escape ruffians.

TRICKY

Rose Crux

Shafir

There are two possible answers. These are either one set of jars 2 full, 6 half-full, and 2 empty and two sets of 4 full, 2 half-full, and 4 empty; or one set of jars 4 full, 2 half-full, and 4 empty, and two sets of 3 full, 4 half-full, and 3 empty.

In each case, you'll note that each son gets as many full jars as empty ones, and that two sons must receive identical distributions.

On The Road

3ft 6" now, and when finished, 10ft 6". If the hole's current depth is x, the man's head is $(5.83 - x)$ feet above the ground now, and when it's 3 times as deep, his head will be twice as far below as it is now, so $(5.83 - 3x) = -2 (5.83 - x)$. Expand that out, so that $5.83 - 3x = -11.66 + 2x$, and simplify to $17.5 = 5x$. That gives $x = 3.5$ft, or 3ft 6". Three times that depth is 10ft 6". His head is (5ft10" - 3ft6" =) 2ft 4" above ground now, and will be (5ft10" - 10ft6" =) 4ft 8" below afterwards.

Scaled

$\odot = 1$. $\mathfrak{D} = 11$. $\yen = 9$. $\mathfrak{P} = 8$.

The Marmo Set

1.75 years, 3.5 years, 5.25 years, 10.5 years and 21 years. We don't know Norina's age, so let's call that 'n'. Then Biagino is 2n, and Erminia is 3n, because her age + Norina's = 2x Biagino's. So when Salvatore enters the equation, the boys' age totals 8n, so Salvatore is 6n. Emily has to be ((2×8n)-3n-n), or 12n. We know Emily is 21, so n=1.75yrs.

TRICKY

Alignment Issues

When the clock shows 8h, 43m and 38s. Aside from 12:00:00, conjunctions occur when the minute hand laps the hour hand on its circuit. There are 12 hours, so while the hour hand makes one circuit, the minute hand makes 12 circuits. It takes more than an hour for the first overlap to occur however, so there are only 11 overlaps before 12:00:00 comes back, and this has to fit exactly into 12 hours.

So the hands overlap every 12/11th of an hour, or every 1 hour, 5 minutes and 27.272 seconds. So multiply by 8 for the next time after 8pm, and you get 8 hours, 43 minutes and 38 seconds. As an aside, the way it works out means that if there is a hand for seconds, all three only come together at exactly 12:00:00.

Calne

In fact, it's reasonably straightforward. If you soak a raw egg in vinegar overnight, the shell will become quite soft and rubbery. Then if you set a small paper fire in the bottle, the oxygen it consumes will pull the egg through the small opening. Once it is in place, wash the bottle out with cold water, which will clear away the burnt paper, and also restore the shell to normal.

high Stakes

The way to win this game – assuming both players can play with perfect skill – is to mirror the opponent's move exactly. It doesn't matter how big the table is, or what size the stakes are. Player A does something, and so long as nothing has gone wrong, Player B will always be able to make an exact mirror-image move.

So the advantage is very much with the player who goes second... But there is one move that cannot be mirrored. That is to place a stake over the exact centre of the table. So if Player A leads with that move, Player B is forced into making a novel move, which Player A can then mirror, and the advantage goes to Player A.

TRICKY

Spot the Difference

Affairs of the heart

It wasn't the woman who had the heart attack.
It was her doctor.

Knight's Move

They meet twice, at midday on the third day (23 miles out from the base), and at the end of the fourth day (34 miles out from the base). Cumulatively, the two men's distances travelled are 0 +10 =10 / 14 + 2 =16 at the end of day 1; 19 / 20 on day 2; 27 / 26 on day 3, the day when Blaise passes Rickard; 34 / 34 on day 4, when Rickard catches back up to Blaise; 40 / 44 on day 5; 45 / 56 on day 6; and 49 / 70 on day 7.

Bundle

The deal is very unfair to Tina. A 10" diameter bundle has an area of 78.5 square inches (5 × 5 × 3.14), while a 5" diameter bundle has a diameter of 19.6 square inches – just a quarter of the 10" one. Gianni should be offering her four bunches, not two.

TRICKY

Three Squared

Think of the pattern as several pieces, as below. Starting at (1), travel anticlockwise around the outside of the design to (2). Jump inside to (3), and perform a loop of the insides. Come back to (3), then switch back to the outside at (2), and go round to (1). Jump inside again to (4) and perform another loop. The entire route has now been walked.

A Merchant of Venice

He deals in timekeeping devices, which range from sundials with no moving parts, through mechanical devices, to hourglasses, which can contain many millions of sand grains. Any of the three might be very small or very big. We also now have electrical clocks of course, and they also fit the conditions, but they wouldn't have been around for a medieval puzzle...

TRICKY

Several Brothers

There are 7 Johnson children, 3 male and 4 female, compared to 5 Wilson children, 2 male and 3 female. Will Johnson has two brothers and four sisters, while his sister has three of each. John Wilson has one brother and three sisters, while his sister has two of each.

TRICKY

The Captive Queen

It is possible, through a series of journeys, to get everyone to the ground: (1) Put the chest in, which goes down. (2) Put her son in, sending him down and the chest back up. (3) Take out the chest, then the daughter gets in & descends, sending the son back up. (4) Take the son out, put the chest in, and then the daughter gets out below, and the chest goes down. (5) The daughter gets back in with chest, the Queen gets in, the Queen descends as her daughter and the chest ascend, the daughter gets out, and the Queen gets out. (6) The chest, still in the basket, goes down, bringing the empty basket back up. (7) Repeat steps (2), (3), and (4), leaving the Queen on the ground with her daughter, and the chest in the basket, while the son is upstairs. (8) The son gets in and descends as the chest ascends. (9) The son gets out to join the family and the chest drops to the ground.

Weighting

6. $(2×10) + (7×8) = (8×2) + (10×x)$. So $10x + 16 = 76$, or $x=6$. The 7 hundredweight load is directly below the pivot, so it can be totally ignored.

TRICKY

Cannon

4564. The most efficient way to stack the balls is in alternating rows, so that they lock together in overlapping layers. Two layers of overlapping balls take up a little over 3.46" rather than 4" – in a hexagonal ABAB lattice, the distance between two rows of A is diameter of the balls D × (sin (120) / sin (30)); 2×1.732=3.464 – so you can fit 13 rows in total into 22.8" of space, and the 14" width gives you 7 balls as the widest row. You can make a largest layer of 85 balls if you have 13 rows alternating 7 and 6 balls per row.

Above it, you can fit an overlapping layer with 12 rows, again alternating 7 and 6 balls, for 78 in total. This pattern can be repeated to a total of 14 layers, 7 of 85 balls and 7 of 78. Together these give us 1,141 balls per crate, or 4,564 total.

Hard Solutions

Chicken

Yes. After 55 seconds, Otto will overtake Bili, having run about 968 feet.

Lovers

They are 29.4 and 19.6 years old. When the man was (2x), the woman was (x). She is now (2x), so (x) time has passed, and the man is (3x). Their combined ages are (5x). 49/5 gives (x) as 9.8. The woman, at (2x) is 19.6y, and the man, at 3x, is 29.4y.

Rose Rows

Yes. Arrange them like so:

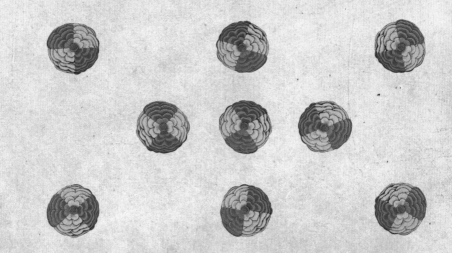

You then have three horizontal rows, one vertical row down the centre. Additionally, each end rose along the top (or, alternatively, the bottom) produces two rows, one leading to the centre of the bottom (top) row via the near-side rose on the centre row, and the other leading to the far side of the bottom (top) row via the central rose. Finally, the centre-top (bottom) rose connects to the two end roses on the bottom (top), via the end roses on the middle row.
3 + 1 + 2 + 2 + 2 = 10.

hARD

The Scarves

Hadise would be considered the best. For rapidity, Hadise to Selime is 5:2, and Hadise to Aysul is 3:4. Since Hadise is the benchmark, let's multiply so Hadise reaches 15 in both cases, so it becomes 15:6 and 15:20. The rapidity scores are in a ratio of 20:15:6 for Aysul, Hadise and Selime in order.

Perform similar calculations for the other qualities. Lightness gives Aysul 5:1 over Hadise and 3:5 to Selime, or 15:3:25 if we take the girls in the same order as lightness.

Warmth tells us that Selime's scarves are four times as good as Aysul's, and Hadise's are three times as good again, so the ratio is 3.75:60:15 in order, standardised to 15 for the girl in common. So now we have three ratios.

Totalling those scores, we arrive at 38.75 for Aysul, 78 for Hadise and 46 for Salime.

Diced Doge

30. There will always be one face that is coloured (a), so let us use that as our standard point for comparing cubes, and rotate (a) to always look at us. The opposite face, (b), has five options. That leaves us with the (effectively) cylindrical band of four faces. As with (a), there will always be one face of this band that is coloured (c), and because the band can rotate, we can standardise (c) pointing up, so the only points of variance are in the other three faces.

Three colours can be distributed six ways (3 x 2 x 1 = 6). Therefore we have 5 varieties for (b), each with 6 options for c-f. 5 x 6 = 30.

The Garden of Winding Paths

Treat the circles radiating outwards as figures of eight. Head down to the inner circle, then around to each pair of radiating circles in turn. Wind around them and back down, then go round to the next. Finish by coming back up the other half of the top pair to return to your start point.

hARD

Carter

Both men saw 19 carts. The westbound cart takes 120 minutes, and the eastbound 180. We need to compare common distances, so take the lowest common multiple, 360, and divide the circuit into that many parts. However far one part is, the westbound track is travelling at 3 parts a minute, with carts spread out one every 45 parts, while the eastbound track is moving at 2 parts a minute, with carts spread 30 parts distant.

Leaving as part of the pattern, for the carters heading in both directions, the inbound cart is 15 minutes away. For the westbound cart, that's a distance of 30 parts and for the eastbound cart, that's 45 parts. Westbound, the carter is travelling 3 parts for each 2 of the incoming cart, so they'll meet ⅗ into the 30-part distance, after he has travelled 18 parts.

Eastbound, the carter is travelling 2:3 over a 45-part distance, so they'll meet ⅖ into his distance – again, after 18 parts. The two men will meet carts after the same distance covered. There are 360 parts to the circuit and a cart every 18, so that's 20 carts, but the last meeting is the return to the depot.

Fill In the Blanks

3 x 1, 2 x 2, 3 x 3, 1 x 4 and 1 x 5. Since there are five spaces and five example digits, the total number of instances must come to ten. Plug in an initial answer, and then repeatedly counting the digits and plugging those back in will bring you to the true answer.

For example, try inputting all 1s. This is clearly false, as totalling across the puzzle, this gives you six 1s and one each of the other four. So try again with 6 1 1 1 1. Still false; you now have 5 1 1 1 1. Which leads > 5 1 1 1 2 > 4 2 1 1 2 > 3 3 1 2 1 > 3 2 3 1 1, which is accurate.

Annual

No. A 1 in 7 chance would be 365/2555. There are 52 weeks and one day in a year, so the chance of it being any particular day is either 364/2555 or 371/2555, depending on which day gets the extra.

To calculate an exact chance, you need a repeating cycle which fits exactly into a number of weeks. Leap years muddy the chances further, adding a second extra day every four years – except once a century, when they do not. So there are 36524 days in a century, which is 5217 weeks and five days.

Every 400 years, the century leap day is allowed, so there are 146097 days in a 400 year cycle, which, finally, is exactly 20871 weeks. So while exactly 1 in 7 of the days in each 400-year cycle relate to each day of the week, for any smaller unit of time the division of days isn't that precise.

hARD

Matching Pairs

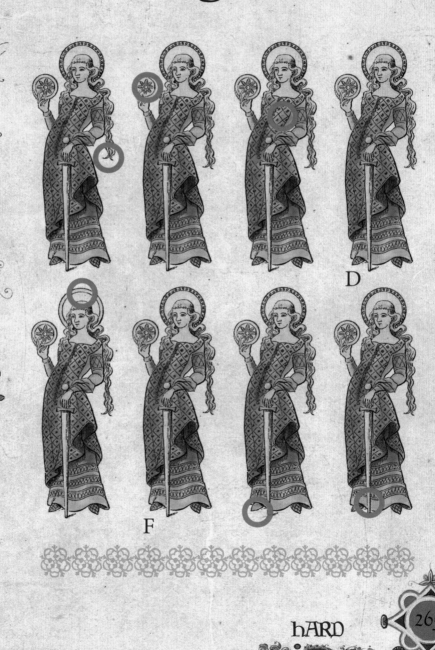

D

F

Toledo

The number 1. Multiply the top row and bottom row and subtract the latter from the former.
16 × 9 = 144; 13 × 11= 143. 144-143=1.

Mathic

73.

hARD

Rhys

He was trapped in a small space underground by a cave-in and died two days later.

Countering

It is better to select a bag at random. Individually, the first bag has a ⅔ chance of holding a white counter and the second bag has a ⅓ chance of you extracting a white counter. Given it's a 50-50 shot at getting either bag, you have a net chance of ½ of retrieving a white counter.

The combined bag contains either WWBB at a ⅔ chance, or WBBB at a ⅓ chance. If WWBB, it's a ½ chance of white; if WBBB, it's a ¼ chance. (⅔ × ½ =) ⅓ + (⅓ × ¼ =) ¹⁄₁₂, so the combined bag has a 5/12 chance of producing a white.

Square Magic

22	47	16	**41**	10	35	4
5	23	48	**17**	42	11	29
30	6	24	**49**	18	36	12
13	**31**	7	**25**	**43**	**19**	**37**
38	14	32	**1**	26	44	20
21	39	8	**33**	2	27	45
46	15	40	**9**	34	3	28

HARD

Players

Snori receives 8 and 1/8th notches, and Rognald the remaining 1 and 7/8ths. The fairest option is to work out how likely it would be for each man to win given the current position, and then divide the prize on that basis. With five games to go, Snori needs to win at least two, or Rognald needs to win at least four.

There are 32 outcomes of the five games, ranging from SSSSS to RRRRR, and in just six of those, Rognald wins four or more of the remaining games. So Rognald has a 3/16 change of winning, and Snori a 13/16 chance. The prize should thus be divided 18.75% to Rognald, and 81.25% to Snori.

The Box

12" × 10" × 8." If Pythagoras' theorem is true for three numbers – a 'Pythagorean Triple' – then it is true for other numbers in the same proportion, which includes those numbers squared.

So multiplying the areas of the top and the side and dividing by the end will give us the square of the length. 120 × 96/80=144, which means the box is 12" in length. 120/12 gives 10" width, and 80/10 gives 8" depth.

hARD

The Cloth

Edward placed the cloth so that it was under a door,
with opposite ends sticking out at either side.

Matching Pairs

F

hARD

The Mysts
of history

383.
The calculation is 647×383
= 247801+592395 = 840196.

Oily

11 pfennigs to Dieter and 2 to Nils.
Nils has gone from 5 pints to 4⅓, a loss of ⅔,
while Dieter has gone from 8 to the same amount,
dropping 3⅔. Multiply the threes out, and you
discover that their losses are in the ratio 11:2,
so their recompense should be too.

Dominicans

Six places ahead, so that if the master is considered number 1, the first person selected is number 7. There is no general equation for solving this type of problem, known as the Josephus Problem; inserting a number and seeing which place remains at the end shows you the offset between the first pick and last person remaining. The technique of "try it and see how many you're out by" or the 'false position method' is generally known as "regula falsi." Everything sounds better in Latin.

hARD

Rupert's Square

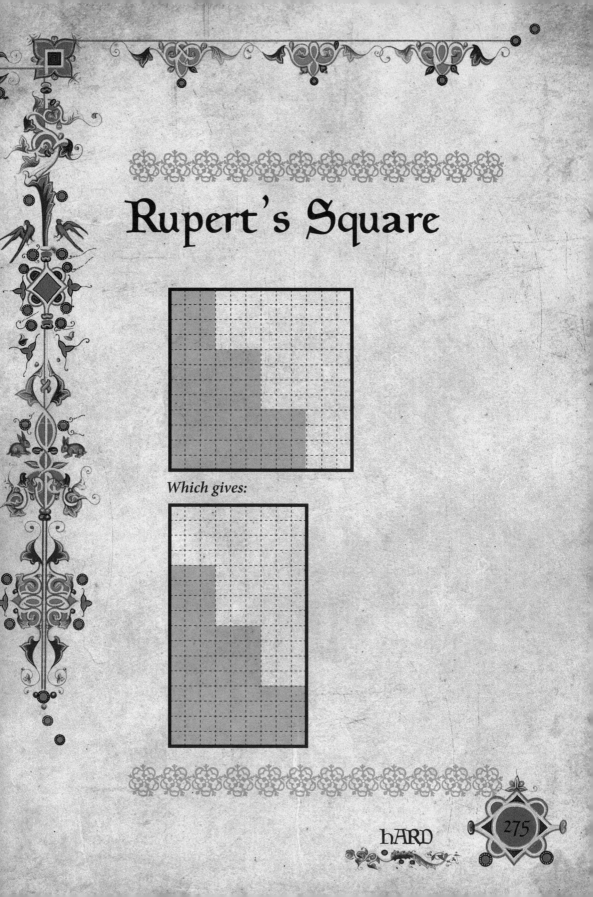

Which gives:

Al hazrad

Munir. The only consistent possibility that gives a definitive answer is if Hamza and Alim are lying.

Very Nice

$79 + 5\frac{1}{3} = 84\frac{2}{3}$.

Curious By Design

64. Opposing pairs of numbers derive the number in the middle – 8^2, 78 - 14 and 16 × 4.

Black Robb

Cambpell's stake was placed just 15 feet from the door of the croft. There was no way to reach the door without being attacked.

Dice

5 & 9 for one player, and 13 & 15 for the other. There are 216 outcomes; six of those outcomes total 5, twenty five total 9, twenty one total 13 and ten total 15.

6 + 25 = 10 + 21 = 31 chances out of 216, or just over a 1/7 chance of winning.

Mathematical Masonry

In each column, multiply the number of stars in the first two rows to give the number of stars in the third row.

Spot the Difference

Savvy

Two. Divide the coins into three stacks of three, and weigh any two. If they are the same, then the third stack holds the counterfeit; if they are different, it is the lighter stack. Take the stack with the counterfeit and again weigh any two of its coins. The lighter is the bad one, or, if the weights are identical, it is the one left over.

Loafing

9.167 loaves. *This is one of those occasions where the answer is arrived at most simply through regula falsi (see the answer to the puzzle Dominicans) – that is, by trying, and seeing how far out you are.*

Trying a 10-loaf gap starting at 1 loaf totals 105 loaves; so long as the first person is receiving something, 10 loaves is just too many. A 9-loaf gap starting at 2 loaves gives 100, but $(2+11)\times7$ [91] =/= [87] (20+29+38). A 9.2-loaf gap starting at 1.6 gives 100, but $(1.6+10.8)\times7$ [86.8] =/= [87.6] (20+29.2+38.4). This is closer, but more importantly, the error has fallen on the other side. At 9 loaves, it was 4 for the smaller shares; at 9.2, it is 0.8 to the larger shares. The proportion 4:0.8 is equal to 5:1, so the balance point we need is 5/6 of the way from 9 to 9.2. Since ⅚ of ⅕ is ⅙, the balance point is 9 and ⅙, or 9.167. Similarly, the size of the smallest share is ⅚ths of the way between 2 and 1.6, or 1.667, with the other shares being 10.833, 20, 29.167 and 38.333.

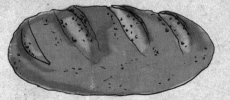

The Urchin

9.6 years old. Break the statements into equations, where x is the boy's age.

$(D - x) = (T - x) / 4$. $D = G / 3$. $x = T/4$. $(x + 4) = (G + 4) / 4$. Multiply up to get rid of divisors and leave just simple terms on the right of each equation, and you have $4D - 3x = T$, $4x = T$, $3D = G$ and $4x + 12 = G$. Combine to remove unknowns, and you get $3D = 4x + 12$ and $4D = 7x$. Combine again, and you'll find that $21x = 16x + 48$, or $x = 48/5 = 9.6$. Similarly, Daisy is 16.8, Tony is 38.4 and Gary is 50.4.

hARD

Scales

♂ = 1.

☉ = 2.

♀ = 3.

☿ = 4.

♃ = 6.

☽ = 8.

Docking

Two men each marry the mother of the other,
presumably after both their fathers have perished
(or absconded under a cloud.) Both men father sons
– Tobias and Harry – with their new wives. Then the
sons are both uncle and nephew to one another, each
being the half-brother of the other's father
(and each son's mother being the other's grandmother).

hARD

Quadruped

16, 10 and 6 half-pfennigs respectively. Note it out in half-pfennigs as $a + (b + c) / 2 = 24$, $b + 2(a+c) / 3 = 24.666$ and $3(a+b) / 4 + c = 25.5$. Multiply it out, so $2a+b+c=48$, $2a+3b+2c = 74$, and $3a+3b +4c = 102$. You then have three simple simultaneous equations. Reorder the first equation for c, substitute into the other two, and you'll get $2a-b = 110$ and $5a+b = 90$; solving that for b will tell you that $110 + 7b = 180$, or $b = 10$. That means $a = 16$, and c in turn $= 6$.

Triptych

$\odot = 27. \; \Psi = 29. \; \mathcal{D} = 31. \; \mathcal{P} = 35. \; \mathcal{J} = 37.$

Cellar

Ernesto lights both ends of one string, and just one end of the other, making sure they aren't touching. When the first has totally burnt out, exactly thirty minutes has passed. He can then light the other end of the second string. It will then burn out in 15 minutes.

hARD

Barras

Only two sets of four numbers which total 100 have the squares of the three smaller numbers summing to the square of the larger. They are 39, 34, 14, 13 and 42, 40, 10, 8. With one year's difference, the former ages are those of the Clough family, while the latter ages are those of the Allsop family.

The Dordonnese Way

☉ = 28. ☽ = 12. ♃ = 17. ♀ = 35.

For more
books like
this please visit:

www.carltonbooks.com

The End